WHAT IT MEANS TO LIVE AS A CHRISTIAN

FOLLOWING JESUS

DOUGLAS SHAW

WITH BAYARD TAYLOR

Gospel Light

VNYS BV 4520 .F65
S43 1999 c.1
CYL406

Gospel Light is an evangelical Christian publisher dedicated to serving the local church. We believe God's vision for Gospel Light is to provide church leaders with biblical, user-friendly materials that will help them evangelize, disciple and minister to children, youth and families.

We hope this Gospel Light resource will help you discover biblical truth for your own life and help you minister to adults. God bless you in your work.

For a free catalog of resources from Gospel Light please contact your Christian supplier or contact us at 1-800-4-GOSPEL *or at* www.gospellight.com.

PUBLISHING STAFF

William T. Greig, Publisher
Dr. Elmer L. Towns, Senior Consulting Publisher
Dr. Gary S. Greig, Senior Consulting Editor
Jill Honodel, Editor
Pam Weston, Assistant Editor
Patti Virtue, Editorial Assistant
Kyle Duncan, Associate Publisher
Bayard Taylor, M.Div., Senior Editor, Theological and Biblical Issues
Barbara LeVan Fisher, Cover Designer
Debi Thayer, Designer

ISBN 0-8307-2416-8

CONTENTS

INTRODUCTION

Why this study? As the decades of the '80s and '90s get relegated to the pages of history books, a silent revolution of religion has been in process. A "bloodless coup," no longer necessitating the finished work of the cross of Jesus Christ for human salvation, has built altars to new gods and belief systems. While many churches are fighting for survival, some of them are closing their doors. While many pray, some have despaired of prayerfully waiting for revival. As the silhouette of church steeples against the sky of many cosmopolitan population centers is being altered by the structures of mosques, Hindu and Buddhist temples and edifices dedicated to cults and the occult, America is slowly but surely being "de-christianized."

The foundational truth of biblical Christianity is being abandoned by many for new religious experiences that are often a repackaging of Eastern mystical religious experiences and the occult. A paradigm shift in the belief systems of Americans has taken place. False religion is masquerading as "truth." A new realization for Christians in America is that they may have lost track of the spiritual condition of other people.

However, it is not a scenario that would be unfamiliar to Noah, Abraham, Moses, Elijah or Paul on Mars Hill—they have all been there before, spectators at the parade of the gods. Jesus has been there all the time. As *the* Light, He shines in darkness and the darkness can never extinguish Him! That is the hope of the Christian. We are believers in an unchanging gospel, despite changing times. We are called to communicate the timeless truth to a lost humanity overshadowed by the ominous sound of a ticking time bomb, hurrying the global village toward God's final hour of judgment.

This study is designed to help you deal with these crucial issues that are pressed into the heart of America. This study is for the spiritual seeker of biblical truth and for the new believer who needs to be appropriately briefed about living as a Christian in today's world. It offers information, inspiration and a call to involvement and to action in a world embroiled in spiritual war. This study is aimed at equipping you for the race that must be run and for the battle that must be won.

Your fellow brother in Christ,
Douglas Shaw

How to Use This Book

This book is designed with believers and seekers in mind. It is flexible enough to be used by individuals who intend to work through this study on their own or in pairs or small groups as a workbook. It is suggested that readers keep a Bible, notebook and pen handy as they cultivate a greater understanding of their lives with Christ as they work their way through this study.

The study is flexible enough to be used in a group setting as well. Each chapter has been created for a weekday Bible study or an adult Sunday School lesson. The leader's guide in the back provides group activities, discussion and interaction to reinforce each lesson, as well as tips on how to lead the class.

Whether you use this study as an individual or in a group setting, you will enter into a transformative, life-giving experience as you learn more of what it means to truly be a Christian.

Keep in mind that we have used the *New International Version* of the *Holy Bible*. Other versions that are used in this study are the *New King James Version* (*NKJV*) and the *New American Standard Bible* (*NASB*). You may, of course, use any reputable version that suits you. However, you will find some translational differences in the fill-in-the blanks sections.

NOTE THAT EACH OF THE SIX CHAPTERS HAS THE FOLLOWING PARTS:

- KEY VERSE—Each session begins with a verse from Scripture that encapsulates the theme of the session.
- BIG LIES—Attitudes and beliefs commonly held in our culture that directly or indirectly deny biblical truth.
- GOD'S TRUTH—The heart of the chapter provides commentary and interaction with Bible verses, that can be used as a workbook or springboard for discussion.
- THOUGHTS FOR REFLECTION—A short illustration or essay that brings out the main point of the lesson.
- CONCLUSION—Concluding thoughts.

- **CLIMBING HIGHER**—Concludes the session with practical application questions and activities to put the lesson into action.

The **LEADER'S GUIDE** provides tips in leading a small or large group Bible study.

BEFORE YOU BEGIN

These six chapters before you are based upon two ancient triads: The belief that the eternal God has always existed in three Persons—God the Father, God the Son and God the Holy Spirit—and the conviction that the most important virtues of the Christian life are faith, hope and love.

This study presumes:
- That God is able to communicate with us and has communicated in many ways, culminating in sending Jesus Christ, God the Son, to be the Savior of the world.
- That the Bible—the 66 books of the Old and New Testaments—is God's written Word and clearly communicates to us the truth about God, His actions in history and His plans to bring history to a close.
- That within each of us is a God-shaped vacuum that can only be filled by our Creator, Jesus Christ.
- That you have a yearning to know what it means to follow Jesus.

STUDY HINTS

1. If you are studying this book on your own, it is suggested that you find a more mature Christian to whom you can go for counsel when you are having difficulty understanding a passage of Scripture or a concept. If you are studying as part of a group, write down your questions or concerns to discuss later with your Bible study leader.
2. Before you begin each chapter, prayerfully ask God's Holy Spirit to teach you and help you understand His Word.
3. As you study, you may come across a concept or question that you do not understand. It is all right to skip the difficult ones. It may become clearer as you continue the chapter. Or you can ask someone else to help you clarify your understanding.
4. Plan on spreading the study over a few days. Don't try to answer all the questions in one sitting. If you are new to looking up and reading Scripture, you may begin to feel overwhelmed with all the new knowledge you are attaining. Give yourself time to meditate on the ideas and concepts you will be taught in this book.

A LIFE-CHANGING JOURNEY BEGINS AS YOU TURN THIS PAGE!

ENJOY THE ADVENTURE!

— ONE —

GOD THE FATHER

KEY VERSE

"For us there is but one God, the Father, from whom all things came and for whom we live." 1 Corinthians 8:6

BIG LIES

- I'm God, you're God, we're all God.
- God is an energy or force that includes both good and evil.
- We all find God in our own way.
- What's true and moral for you may not be true and moral for me.
- God and the spirit world are just illusions.
- The physical universe is all there is.

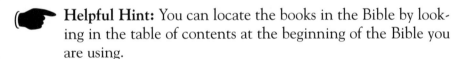 **Helpful Hint:** You can locate the books in the Bible by looking in the table of contents at the beginning of the Bible you are using.

GOD'S TRUTH

GOD WANTS TO BE YOUR FATHER

God earnestly desires to be your Father so that you can have an intimate relationship with Him. God loves you more deeply than you can imagine.

Tragically for many people, speaking of God as Father immediately presents difficulties. Those who have had bad experiences with their fathers may be hindered from perceiving God's love for them or from emotionally connecting with God, especially if their fathers didn't communicate love to them in ways they could understand.

1. What kind of relationship did/do you have with your own father? How might your relationship with your earthly father affect your relationship with your heavenly Father?

 Action Step: If your relationship with your father was painful, difficult or nonexistent, before you go any further in this study, ask God's Holy Spirit to reveal to you the areas of pain that you have with your earthly father, and pray that this past experience might not block your relationship with your heavenly Father. His Holy Spirit will help you let go of your negative emotions toward your father.

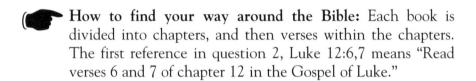 **How to find your way around the Bible:** Each book is divided into chapters, and then verses within the chapters. The first reference in question 2, Luke 12:6,7 means "Read verses 6 and 7 of chapter 12 in the Gospel of Luke."

2. Read Luke 12:6,7. Is it hard for you to believe that God could be interested in every area of your life? Why or why not?

3. According to Galatians 4:3-6, we are either _____ of the principles of this world (sin) or we are _____ of God. This passage points out the fact that becoming children of God is not automatic at our physical birth; it requires us to choose to become His children.

Jesus, the only person who has ever had a perfect relationship with God the Father, called God "Abba, Father" (Mark 14:36). In Jesus' time little children would greet their daddies and papas as "Abba." What does it mean to you that you can call the Creator of the universe "Daddy"?

GOD THE FATHER REVEALS HIMSELF

One of the big lies many people believe about God is that we can't really know Him. This lie puts God "in a box" and infers that the God who created the entire universe is incapable of communicating any truth to those whom He has created. However, according to the Bible, God is continually revealing Himself to us.

The first five books of the Bible (the Torah) were written by Moses, who had been educated in Pharaoh's royal house. Moses was fully aware of the many tribal deities worshiped by the Egyptians and the surrounding peoples. However, these gods, goddesses, spirits and ancestors were all limited in various ways. Our Creator God is unlimited in His attributes and abilities.

4. Read Genesis 1:1. Why would Genesis 1:1 have been so revolutionary in such a setting? Do you think Genesis 1:1 is revolutionary in our present-day culture? Why or why not?

AS OUR CREATOR

We often hear phrases such as "All humans are divine" and that we need to "recognize our divinity as human beings." In fact, some people even come right out and say, "I am God."

5. Read Job 38:1-7. Previous to this passage, Job is questioning why God has allowed him to suffer the loss of his family, his property and his livelihood. God actually uses sarcasm to convey an important message to Job. What is that message?

   How much credit can you take for creating and designing the heavens and the earth?

6. Read Psalm 19:1-4 and Romans 1:19,20. These verses tell us that God has given abundant evidence of Himself in the natural world.

In what ways have you seen specific evidence of God's existence in the world around you?

For many years the platform of the National Association of Biology Teachers (NABT) read, "The diversity of life on Earth is the outcome of evolution: an unsupervised, impersonal, unpredictable and natural process." In other words, the natural world is merely the combination of chance and matter. Even a popular children's book on nature states that nature "is all that IS, or WAS or EVER WILL BE."[1]

What do these statements say about the ultimate meaning of life? How do they contradict the Genesis and Job passages in questions 4 and 5?

As Our Moral Authority
No doubt you have heard the phrase, "You can't legislate morality." Let's see if this statement applies to God.

7. Read Romans 2:14,15. What does your conscience tell you about right and wrong and facing the judgment of God? (**Note:** The term "Gentiles" refers to people who are not Jewish and, therefore, do not have the benefit of a clear explanation of the moral law in the Old Testament.)

We often hear that right and wrong are purely determined by the individual person, or that right and wrong are merely social conventions or the means by which those in power control others. How do these views contrast with what you know deep down inside?

As a Personal, Holy and Loving God

8. Read 1 John 1:5. This is only one of many passages that speak of the pristine holiness of God. According to this passage, is there any mixture of good and evil in God at all?

Have you ever done something that you knew was wrong? How did you know it was wrong? Why did you do it anyway?

Contrast 1 John 1:5 with the belief that the ultimate power of the universe is a force that has an evil (dark) and a good (light) side.

If the ultimate power of the universe is both evil and good, then is our world essentially a moral or an amoral (nonmoral) place? Can an impersonal force or energy love you personally?

THROUGH HIS WORD

Read 2 Timothy 3:16 and John 1:1-3,14. In addition to the natural world and our conscience, God reveals Himself through His written Word, the Bible, and in Jesus Christ, the personified Word of God.

9. What do you think you can learn about God from the Bible? What other methods have you used to learn about God?

Why would regular, consistent reading of the Bible be important for getting to know and love God as your Father?

WHO WE ARE IN RELATION TO GOD

We're not God; we can never be divine in the same way God is. But this does not mean that we are unimportant to God or that He is indifferent to us.

CREATED IN HIS IMAGE

10. Read Genesis 1:26,27. What does it mean to be created in the "image" of God. What responsibilities might it involve?

Some have claimed that people create God in their own image. Do you agree or disagree and why?

One of the most awesome aspects of being created in God's image is the capacity to relate to God personally because He is near and not just "everywhere" (see Jeremiah 23:23,24).

INVITED TO INTIMACY

11. How do you develop a friendship with another person? How can you relate these aspects of friendship to developing a conversational relationship with God, your loving Father?

12. Read Deuteronomy 6:4,5 and Matthew 22:37. The Deuteronomy passage is quoted in Jewish synagogues every time worship takes place. The Matthew passage is Jesus' affirmation of the Deuteronomy passage. What does a person do who loves God with all his or her heart, soul, mind and strength?

    Read Deuteronomy 6:13. How is it possible to love and fear God at the same time?

ACCOUNTABLE TO GOD

In Exodus 20:1-17 God gives us clear and specific guidance on how to go about obeying, loving and fearing Him. Notice that these 10 items are not called God's "opinions" or "suggestions" about what is right and wrong. They are His *commandments*.

The Ten Commandments have been critically important for establishing a standard for morality and law in western culture, yet very few people today can name more than one or two of them.

13. Summarize each of the Ten Commandments from Exodus 20:1-17 in your own words:

    I.

    II.

    III.

    IV.

    V.

    VI.

    VII.

    VIII.

    IX.

    X.

14. Read Psalm 24:1. If God is the Creator of you, all the peoples and cultures of the world and indeed the whole universe, does He have the right to demand exclusive worship from you? Is God being intolerant by demanding exclusive worship? Do you have the right to create your own religious path apart from the God who created you? Why or why not?

As Creator and Owner of the universe and of you, does God have the right to determine what is right and wrong? Is God intolerant by demanding that we respect and obey His laws? Do you have the right to "create your own values" without reference to what God has revealed as right and wrong? Explain your answer.

GOD HAS AN ADVERSARY

Where does the evil in the world come from? The Bible says that God has an adversary called Satan, the devil, an angel created by God and inferior to God, who led a rebellion of angels (now called "demons") against God (see Revelation 12:7). Satan knows that the only reason we are created is to worship God. And since he hates God and the people God has created, he will use any means at his disposal to subvert God's purpose and deceive them into worshiping anything but the One True God.

15. Read Genesis 3:1-7. What did the serpent (later revealed as Satan, see Revelation 12:9) imply about God by his questions to Eve?

    To what human desires did the serpent appeal?

    What is appealing about disobeying God?

16. Read John 8:44 and 1 Peter 5:8. What is the devil/Satan called in these verses?

    According to 1 John 3:8 and 4:1-4, why should believers in Jesus Christ *not* fear Satan? What is the Christian's defense against Satan?

17. The Bible provides plenty of warning against seeking spiritual truth or experiences apart from the worship of the One True God. Match the following deceptive practices with their corresponding references.

    a. Deuteronomy 4:19   Pursuing occult practices

    b. Deuteronomy 18:10-12   Returning to worship of other gods

    c. Judges 2:16-19   Worshiping carved or foreign gods

    d. Jeremiah 2:25-28   Worshiping creation rather than the Creator

18. Read John 10:10. Have you ever been robbed, betrayed, ripped off, or thought someone was trying to fool you? How did that make you feel?

The emotions you experienced are *not* representative of the life God wants you to experience. Satan is a rip-off artist, worse than the vilest sociopath.

Reread John 10:10. Contrast Satan's plan to what Jesus wants to give us.

THOUGHTS FOR REFLECTION

Down through the centuries, many have believed that the God of the universe is very impersonal. Bible passages such as Psalm 139 confirm that God created each human being, has total knowledge about every person and continually projects positive thoughts toward them. It is only since the early '90s that scientific research has verified that every human being has his/her own unique DNA. God knows who we are and He has specific plans for each one of us. It is no wonder that Jesus categorically stated to His followers that if the Father in heaven knows about every sparrow that falls to the ground, surely He cares for every human being as well (see Matthew 10:29).

At the end of his life, Jean-Paul Sartre, perhaps the century's greatest atheistic philosopher, penned this poignant statement: "I often wonder what kind of love affair I could have had with God."[2] How sad! How would it feel to be at the end of your life regretting that you had not made the investment to learn to love God with all your heart, soul, mind and strength?

CONCLUSION

Surely we cannot understand all that God is, but that does not prevent us from being in relationship with Him. Just as a child does not fully understand his/her parents, the child nonetheless has a relationship with his/her mother and father. God is not a distant god. God has created us to be in relationship with Him.

What the Bible reveals about God transcends the spiritual search of any one human being. If we put God in our own box, the Bible may even offend us culturally and spiritually.

Atheists say there is no God, but the Bible calls such a person a fool (see Psalm 14:1). Agnostics say no one can know if there is a God, but the Bible teaches that God has communicated to humanity in many understandable ways (see Romans 1:19,20). New Agers say there are many gods and that we are all gods. From a biblical viewpoint this is blasphemy (see Exodus 20:3,4; 1 Corinthians 8:6). Astrologers say that the way to get in touch with the universe is to understand how the movements of the stars and planets direct events on earth. God explicitly forbids such practices (see Deuteronomy 4:19). Occultists believe in the channeling of spirits of the dead, but the Bible denounces such practices (see Deuteronomy 18:10-12).

The truth that there is one true God means that there *are* absolute truths. When Jesus showed His disciples how to pray, He told them to pray to "our Father in heaven" (Matthew 6:9). This means that God is our protector, our provider *and* our loving and heavenly Father as well. By the way, calling God our Father is not a slight on motherhood. Isaiah 49:15 reveals that God's heart is more compassionate than that of a mother for her nursing child. Likewise, Matthew 23:37 shows us a picture of God longing to gather His children together "as a hen gathers her chicks under her wings."

The One True God exists. He is and has always existed as God the Father, God the Son and God the Holy Spirit, the Holy Trinity. He has made Himself known to humanity through the person of Jesus Christ. God is holy. Worship of any other god amounts to false religion which will incur God's wrath. Why? Because He alone has made salvation available to all humanity. When we, His children, acknowledge Him as our heavenly Father as expressed in Jesus Christ, we begin a love relationship with Him that lasts for all time and eternity.

CLIMBING HIGHER

A. Write at least one way you can honor God the Father this week in each of the following aspects of your life:

Heart/feelings

Will/desires

Mind/thoughts

B. Read and meditate on Psalm 139. Write down the thoughts that come to mind as you meditate on these verses. Find one verse in this passage that especially speaks to you and do one of the following:

Write the verse you've chosen on a 3x5-inch index card and put it in a prominent place where you will read it often this week.

Explain in writing why this verse is meaningful to you.

C. Take a 10-minute walk, notice the beauty and marvel at the complexities of this natural world. Thank the God who is the Father of all creation and who also desires to be your heavenly Father.

 Action Step: Have you ever gotten down on your knees and thanked God for sending Jesus and for the incredible privilege of being redeemed (rescued) from your sin and adopted into God's family so that now you can call the God of the universe "Daddy"?

 How to Start Reading the Bible: The Bible is divided into two major sections. The Old Testament covers creation, the history of Israel and God's people and the expectation of a coming Messiah. The New Testament covers the life, death and resurrection of Jesus Christ, the Messiah; the beginning of the Church and the expectation of the second coming of the Messiah.

A good place to start reading the Bible would be in the Gospel of John, the fourth book of the New Testament.

Notes:
1. Stan and Jan Berenstain, *The Berenstain Bears' Nature Guide* (New York: Random House Books for Young Readers, 1984).
2. Jean-Paul Sartre and Benny Levy, *Hope Now: The 1980 Interviews* (Chicago: University of Chicago Press, 1996).

~ Two ~

GOD THE SON, JESUS CHRIST

KEY VERSES

"Therefore God exalted him to the highest place and gave him the name that is above every name, that at the name of Jesus every knee should bow, in heaven and on earth and under the earth, and every tongue confess that Jesus Christ is Lord, to the glory of God the Father." Philippians 2:9-11

BIG LIES

- Jesus Christ is one of many ways to God.
- Jesus Christ was a great prophet, like Mohammed or Buddha.
- The Christ is already within you; you just need to realize it.
- Christ is the universal, cosmic spirit that guides human consciousness in its spiritual evolution.
- You can be in harmony with the universe without Christ.
- Jesus was a clever faith healer that Christians turned into a god.

GOD'S TRUTH

Religion is man's best effort to reach God. The Christian faith is God's best effort to reach us through His Son, Jesus Christ. Who is this Man who has had such an immense influence on human history?

- Jesus was a first-century Jew, born 2,000 years ago in Roman-occupied Palestine, in what is now the modern state of Israel.

- Jesus grew up in the village of Nazareth (see Luke 4:16), a town with a bad reputation (see John 1:46).
- His earthly father Joseph (see Luke 3:23) was a carpenter (see Matthew 13:55).
- Jesus followed His father's trade until He left to begin teaching (see Mark 6:3).
- Even as a child, Jesus could hold His own with scholars of Jewish law (see Luke 2:43-49).

A JEWISH RABBI

When Jesus was about 30 years old, He began His public ministry.

1. Read John 1:38. How did the two disciples address Jesus? What does this term mean?

   Many people try to squeeze Jesus into cultural molds or preconceived notions that completely extract Him from His place in first-century Judaism as an itinerant Jewish rabbi. Why do you think this happens?

2. Several times in Matthew 5 (see vv. 21,22,27,28,31-34,38,39), Jesus says, "You have heard it said…, but I say to you." Read Matthew 7:13-29. Normally, when rabbis argued about how to interpret God's Law they would appeal to the authority of famous rabbis. What is different about Jesus? What does Jesus rest His authority upon?

3. According to Matthew 7:28,29, how did people react to Jesus' teaching?

MUCH MORE THAN A JEWISH RABBI!

HIS BIRTH

4. According to Matthew 1:18-25, what was unusual about Jesus' conception? How does that affect your understanding of who Jesus is?

You can read the other supernatural events surrounding the birth of Christ as recounted in Luke 1—2 and Matthew 2.

HIS MIRACLES

It wasn't only Jesus' words that were uniquely powerful. His deeds demonstrated beyond any doubt that He was much more than an average rabbi. A miracle may be defined as God doing what only He can do.

5. Read Mark 1:23-28. What did the evil spirit/demon say about Jesus? Why were the people who witnessed this miracle so amazed?

6. Besides driving evil spirits out of the demon-possessed, Jesus performed many other miracles. What do the following miracles demonstrate about Jesus' abilities? Match the verses by drawing a line.

    a. Matthew 8:1-3   power over nature

    b. Matthew 8:14,15   ability to multiply resources

    c. Matthew 9:1-8   power over paralysis

    d. Matthew 9:18,19,23-26   power over death

    e. Mark 4:37-41   cured incurable diseases

    f. Mark 6:34-44   cured ordinary illnesses

What were the different reactions to Jesus' miracles?

SUPERNATURAL KNOWLEDGE

7. Read Matthew 20:17-19 and 26:1,2. What do these verses indicate?

Even though Jesus knew beforehand that He was going to die a horrible and shameful death on the Cross, He went ahead with it anyway. Why did He do that? (See Hebrews 12:2; Romans 5:6-8.)

THE NAMES AND TITLES OF JESUS

Jesus' names and titles also reveal that He was much more than just a rabbi, prophet or religious teacher.

"GOD WITH US"

8. Read Matthew 1:21-23. What are the two names mentioned in these verses?

The name "Jesus" is *Yeshua* in Hebrew. It means "Yahweh saves." Yahweh is the personal name of God (see Exodus 3:14). The name *Immanuel* refers to a deliverer who would be "God with us," a prophecy made about 750 years before Christ (see Isaiah 7:14).

MESSIAH

Read John 1:41. Christ (from the Greek) and Messiah (from the Hebrew) both mean "the Anointed One," a title referring to the installation ceremonies of priests and kings in ancient Israel who were anointed with oil as a sign of appointment by God.

9. Read Psalm 2. This psalm is messianic, prophetically speaking of the coming King and Messiah. What does this passage say about the coming Messiah?

SUFFERING SERVANT

10. Read Isaiah 53:3-6. In this prophetic passage Christ is referred to as the suffering Servant. What does the Servant do in this passage?

SON OF GOD

11. What is the central truth of Matthew 16:13-17? Who revealed this truth to Peter?

One of the central aspects of Jesus' self-understanding was His completely unique relationship with His heavenly Father. According to Matthew 3:16,17, what was God's attitude toward Jesus?

12. Read John 3:16-18. What was God's purpose in sending His Son into the world?

SAVIOR OF THE WHOLE WORLD

13. Read John 4:19-26 and 39-42. In verses 25 and 26, how does Jesus describe Himself? In verse 42, what do the villagers conclude?

If Jesus really is the Savior of the *whole world*, what are the implications for His followers?

THE WORD

14. Read John 1:1-3,14. The term "the Word" here refers to the visible expression of the invisible God. Who is verse 14 talking about

when it says "the Word became flesh"? What astounding claims are made about the Word in these verses?

The Way, the Truth, the Life

15. Read John 14:5-11. What is Jesus claiming in these words to His disciples?

Lord of All

The Early Church was made up almost entirely of monotheistic Jews who had been trained from the time they were born that there is only one God, and He alone is to be worshiped. Yet on the basis of their experiences of Jesus' life, death, resurrection and continuing activity among them, these Jewish believers came to understand God in a revolutionary new way.

16. Read Philippians 2:9-11. In the New Testament Jesus is called Lord 700 times and Savior 25 times. If Jesus really is your Lord and Savior, what should this mean in your everyday life?

 Action Step: Is Jesus primarily your Savior, or your Lord? Or is He both? If He is your Savior, what has He saved you from? If He is your Lord, is He Lord of your whole life? Often when we accept Jesus as Lord and Savior, we do not fully comprehend what that means. Sometimes we accept Him only as our Savior and neglect to make Him Lord of our whole life. What are you holding back from Him right now? What area of your life is He not allowed to touch? Take the opportunity to prayerfully commit your *whole* life to Him right now.

17. What do these many titles of Jesus mean to you? Which is the most meaningful and why?

SECOND PERSON OF THE TRINITY

18. In Matthew 28:19 Jesus identifies three distinct Persons whom He asks the disciples to acknowledge when they baptized new believers. Who are these three Persons?

The eternal God has always existed in three Persons: God the Father, God the Son and God the Holy Spirit. This concept will be further explored in chapter 3. **Note:** See page 109 for additional names of Jesus.

THE NECESSITY OF THE CROSS

In the Old Testament, God instructed His people that to approach Him, sin had to be acknowledged and paid for with blood. This resulted in a whole sacrificial system described at length in the book of Leviticus. The reason such drastic measures were required was to show the seriousness of sin and that it involves the rejection of friendship with God and is therefore the worst possible evil, leading to all other evil.

Some people get extremely offended at the message of the Cross. One current highly placed church official has even published his opinion that "the cross as sacrifice is a barbarian idea based on primitive concepts and must be dismissed."

19. Why do you think this central tenant of the Bible and the Early Church offends this fellow's religious sensibilities so much?

The Bible teaches that, yes, the Cross is barbaric, it is extreme, it is offensive, it is a scandal—to human pride. But the Bible also explains that repairing the damage done by human sin requires extreme measures (see Hebrews 9:22). Wars, cruelty, greed, pride, oppression, exploitation, racism, slavery, hopelessness—all can be laid at the door of sin.

20. Read Luke 24:25,26 and Acts 17:2,3. The core proclamation of the Bible and the Early Church is the death, resurrection and ascension of Jesus Christ. Do these verses imply that the Cross was optional?

21. Read Romans 3:23 and 6:23 and complete the following. "For all have _____ and fall short of the _____ of God. For the wages of sin is _____, but the _____ of God is _____ life in Christ Jesus our Lord."

To "sin" means to disobey, to rebel against God, to seek to be independent, to create your own values without reference to God, and to rely on your own wisdom. The attitude of sin separates us from God and leads to all the various sins prohibited in God's commandments.

22. Take another look at the Ten Commandments in the last chapter (p. 15). Look at commandment IX—you shall not lie or give false testimony. Have you ever lied?

    Read Matthew 5:21,22 and compare it with commandment VI. What does Jesus say about harboring anger toward "your brother"? Does that seem too extreme to you?

    Read Matthew 5:27,28 and compare it with commandment VII. What does Jesus say about lusting after another person? Why did Jesus place such importance on our thoughts, and not just our deeds?

    By the way, how are you doing on the other commandments? Where else might you be sinning in thought, if not in deed? James 2:10 warns us that if we break even one law, we are guilty of breaking all of them. What does that tell you about the seriousness of our sins and the need for Jesus' death on the Cross?

23. The following passages outline the ways that sin affects us:

    Read Proverbs 16:2,5,25. If you have convinced yourself that you
    are doing the good and right thing, while you are actually doing
    what displeases God, what has happened?

    In Mark 7:18-23 Jesus defines the meaning of being clean or
    unclean before God. What activities does He list as unclean?
    Where does this uncleanness come from?

    Read John 8:31-36. If you sin, can you free yourself from sinning by
    your own power? What hope does this passage give you?

    Read Ephesians 2:1-3. Describe the condition of the people in this
    passage. How serious is their condition?

    According to Ephesians 2:4-6, what promise has God given those
    who believe and accept His gift?

Contrast the sober but realistic view of humanity in this section with
the idea that everyone is basically good and that bad people are the
result of the evil in society and the environment. Reinhold Niebuhr
(1892-1971) said concerning the twentieth century's bloody legacy of
well over 100 million deaths—two world wars, the Communist gulags
and policies of forced starvation, purges, and genocides—that never
have so many died for the principle that man is basically good!

24. Read 1 John 1:5-10. What is the hardest thing for us to admit to
    ourselves and to God? What is the only thing that can cleanse us
    from our sin?

25. Read 2 Corinthians 5:21. What did Jesus become at the Cross? And what did we gain from His death?

Jesus not only paid the penalty for our sin, but He paved the way to restore us to full humanity. What would be an appropriate response to such overwhelming kindness and mercy?

 Action Step: Read Mark 1:15. To repent *emotionally* means to be grieved at the damage your sin has caused to others and yourself. To repent *behaviorally* is to turn your back on sin and your face toward God. Have you truly repented, both emotionally and behaviorally? Has the enormity of your sin caused you great sorrow? Has your behavior been changed as a result?
Read 1 John 1:8,9. What must you do to repent? What does God promise us when we confess? For what do you need to confess and ask His forgiveness? Do it now!

JESUS' VICTORY OVER SIN, DEATH AND SATAN

The Cross was the most profound statement God could have made to demonstrate His great love for us. But there's more. Jesus rose from the dead and ascended to the right hand of God the Father (see Matthew 28:1-10; Mark 16:1-7; Luke 22:69; 24:45-51; Acts 1:1-9).

26. Read Colossians 1:19,20 and 2:13-15. Describe what Christ has accomplished through His death on the cross in these passages. What has Christ reconciled? Over what is He triumphant?

27. Read Ephesians 1:18,19 and 2:4-7. List all the things God has done for us through Christ's death and resurrection.

What does it mean to "be raised up with Him" and "seated with Him" (v. 6) in the heavenly realms? (For further study see Romans 6:4,5; Galatians 5:24; Colossians 3:1-3.)

28. Read 1 John 3:8. What was the purpose for which Jesus came?

Through the Cross and resurrection of Jesus, Satan's power has been irreversibly broken, and eventually Satan will be totally defeated (see Revelation 20:10,14,15).

 Action Step: Read Romans 10:9,10. If you have never made a profession of your faith in Jesus Christ as Lord and Savior of your life, here is a simple outline of what to do:

> Accept the fact that you are a sinner and need God's grace.
> Believe that Jesus died for your sins and God raised Him from the dead.
> Confess your sins to God and repent of them; also, confess your faith in Christ to others.
> Decide to follow Jesus Christ as Lord and Savior of your life.

THOUGHTS FOR REFLECTION

In India, a young Hindu who made a decision to follow Jesus Christ was ridiculed by a skeptical Hindu. "You mean to say you actually believe that Jesus was 'born of a virgin'? If you can explain that to me, I too will become a Christian."

The convert to Christianity prayerfully thought about his answer for a moment. Then he replied, "You see that black cow out there in the field? If you can explain to me how that black cow eats green grass and gives white milk, I will explain to you the virgin birth."

The Hindu was silenced.

The natural world is full of great mysteries. What is an atom, really? Where did life come from? How does a cow make milk? How much greater a mystery is the God who designed, created and is far above the heavens and the earth, who humbled Himself in human history to the startling extent of taking on human flesh and dying on a cruel cross—all to lift us out of the humiliating degradation of sin and to make us royal heirs in His family? (See Psalm 113 and compare it with Philippians 2:5-11; Ephesians 2:4,5.) If Jesus had been a mere man, He could in no way have fully revealed God. Jesus was not only a fully authentic human being—living the only perfect life ever lived—He was also God. As 1 Timothy 2:5 says, Jesus was the one mediator between God and humanity.

CONCLUSION

Jesus Christ came to earth in the form of a man to reveal God to humanity. Why? Because creation had fallen into the snare of sin, unable to redeem itself. To provide salvation, it was necessary for Him, the sinless Lamb of God, to die a sacrificial death on the Cross. He died, was buried and rose again from the dead. His resurrection opens the door of opportunity and hope to anyone who will believe in Him to have eternal life for now and for eternity. But that's not all. God's ultimate plan includes the restoration of both heaven and earth. Through Christ, a Christian believer is forgiven, cleansed from sin and empowered by God's Spirit to live the Christian life and become more like Him. The Christian is made "complete" in Christ.

CLIMBING HIGHER

A. Write down three titles for Jesus Christ that are especially meaningful to you. Share specifically why each title has personal significance for you.

B. Read and meditate on John 1:1-14. Write down the thoughts that come to mind as you meditate on these verses.

Find one verse in John 1:1-14 that especially speaks to you and do one of the following:

Write the verse on a 3x5-inch card and put it in a prominent place where you can read it often this week.

Explain in writing why this verse is meaningful to you.

C. Find a quiet spot where you can think about what you have learned in this study and about the fruitless search you were on before you met Jesus Christ. Offer a prayer of thanksgiving for who Jesus is and what He means to you now.

 Action Step: Read 1 Corinthians 11:23-26. Part of the Early Church's response was to remember Christ's sacrifice by breaking bread and drinking the cup in a ceremony called the Eucharist, or "Thanksgiving." Next time you take Communion or participate in the Lord's Supper with other believers in Jesus, prepare your heart to fully give God thanks for His mercy and kindness to you in Christ Jesus.

~ THREE ~

GOD THE HOLY SPIRIT

KEY VERSES

"When He, the Spirit of truth, has come, He will guide you into all truth; for He will not speak on His own authority, but whatever He hears He will speak; and He will tell you things to come. He will glorify Me, for He will take of what is Mine and declare it to you." John 16:13,14 (*NKJV*)

BIG LIES

- The "divine light" within you is all the spiritual guidance you need.
- All religions are basically the same.
- The soul is recycled through many physical bodies on the way to perfection.
- Spiritual guidance is available from psychics, astrologers or spirits living in natural objects.
- Follow your bliss, wherever it leads.
- The spiritual world is nothing but speculation and superstition.

GOD'S TRUTH

The Holy Spirit of God has already been working on you for a long time. He has been working throughout your life to bring you to Christ and into deeper intimacy with Him.

Many people today are experimenting with alternative and nontraditional spiritual paths. Many think they have already tried Christianity—i.e., "traditional religion"—and found it lacking. But

God's Holy Spirit continues to appeal to you to make Jesus Christ your Lord and to follow Him only.

WHO THE HOLY SPIRIT IS *NOT!*
There is much confusion over the question *Who is the Holy Spirit?* Because of this it is necessary to make some general statements about who the Holy Spirit is *not.*

- The Holy Spirit is not an impersonal force, cosmic vibration or celestial harmony. He is not an "it."
- The Holy Spirit is not a mixture of good and evil, or of the light and dark sides of an impersonal "force" (see Acts 26:18); rather, the Holy Spirit is holy, righteous, pure and absolutely good.
- The Holy Spirit is not an absolutely inconceivable and unspeakable mystery; rather, the Holy Spirit is a revealer to those who are seeking God (see 1 Corinthians 2:12,13) and a concealer to those who are rebelling against God (see 1 Corinthians 1:18,19).
- The truth the Holy Spirit brings to us is not disorderly, inconsistent and contradictory; rather, it is part of the whole truth that God alone knows because God alone is all-knowing (see 1 Corinthians 2:10,11).

WHO THE HOLY SPIRIT *IS!*
There are many ways in which the Bible indicates that the Holy Spirit has the full attributes of God.

1. Like God the Father and God the Son, the Holy Spirit was present and active in the beginning when the world was created. What phrase in Genesis 1:2 indicates the presence of God's Spirit at the creation of the world?

What do the following verses say about the existence of:

The Father—Psalm 90:2

The Son—Hebrews 13:8

The Holy Spirit—Hebrews 9:14

The mystery of one God eternally existing in Three Persons is beyond human comprehension. Some have tried to illustrate the idea, but no illustration completely captures the mystery of the Trinity.

The concept of three-in-one can be illustrated in some everyday images.
- Water: liquid, steam and ice
- A triangle: three connected lines make up one figure
- A three-dimensional object: height, width, depth
- A human being: body, soul and spirit

Read Isaiah 9:6; Mark 1:9-11; John 14:7-11,16,17; Acts 1:4,5. What do these passages tell you about the partnership of the Trinity?

2. Read Ephesians 4:30. The Holy Spirit of God can be grieved just as God the Father is saddened by sin (see Genesis 6:5,6). Grieving implies emotional capacity, such as can only come from a personality. If the Holy Spirit were a cosmic impersonal force, could He be "grieved"?

Have you ever done anything that "grieved" God? How did you feel afterward?

3. Read Psalm 139:7,8. What divine characteristic is attributed to the Holy Spirit in these verses? What is the connection between God's presence and God's Holy Spirit in this passage?

In what ways have you tried to flee from God's presence?

THE PROMISE OF THE FATHER

The Old Testament promised that God would send His Holy Spirit to the earth in a new way at the coming of the Messiah.

4. Read Isaiah 61:1-3 (written about 750 B.C.) and Luke 4:14-21. What was the Messiah enabled to do through the power of the Holy Spirit?

5. Read Acts 1:4-8. How did Jesus describe the Holy Spirit in these verses?

Read Acts 1:8. The promise of the Father, the Holy Spirit, would empower the disciples to do what?

The progression from Jerusalem, Judea and Samaria and to the ends of the earth describes the expanding movement of the Early Church. The rest of the book of Acts follows the work of the Holy Spirit in this phenomenal expansion.

6. According to Matthew 3:11, John the Baptist had forseen a baptism of fire and the Holy Spirit. How does his prophetic vision compare with Acts 2:1-13?

7. Read Acts 2:16-21. Peter had the privilege of preaching the first sermon of the Church. What does he declare about the power of the Holy Spirit? (Also see Joel 2:28-32.)

Read Acts 2:33 and complete the following:

Jesus was _____ to the right hand of God. He received from the Father the Holy Spirit, and had _____ _____ the Holy Spirit which they were presently experiencing.

The Book of Acts strings together an amazing narrative of how the promise of the Father, the Holy Spirit, worked through the Early Church. Similarly, the promised Holy Spirit of the Father is for today. God wants His people to fully experience the promise and the gifts of His Holy Spirit.

WHAT DOES THE HOLY SPIRIT *DO*?

The Holy Spirit is the energy of God working to reveal who God is. The Old Testament recognized that God's purposes are accomplished "'not by [human] might, nor by [human] power, but by my Spirit,' says the LORD Almighty" (Zechariah 4:6). Similarly, the New Testament shows that from first to last the Holy Spirit enables the Christian to serve God and others (see Acts 4:29-31).

To the degree that we cooperate with the Holy Spirit will be the degree to which our lives reflect God's light to others.

8. According to John 16:13,14 (the key verses), what is the main purpose of the Holy Spirit?

The following subtitles show how all the other things that the Holy Spirit does support His main purpose as stated in John 16:13,14—to glorify Jesus Christ by making Him known.

CONVICTION

The conviction of the Holy Spirit tells us that something in our lives is not right with God.

9. In John 16:7-11, Jesus said that after He went away (returned to His Father) the Helper/the Counselor would come. Complete the following from verse 8:

When He [the Helper/the Counselor/Holy Spirit] has come, He will _____ the world of _____, of _____, and of _____.

What does it mean to convict someone?

Have you ever experienced the conviction of the Holy Spirit? What occurred?

CONVERSION

10. Read John 3:1-8. Jesus told Nicodemus (in verse 3) "No one can see the kingdom of God unless he is _____ _____."

According to verses 5 and 6, who brings about this new birth?

11. Read Ephesians 1:13,14. At conversion, we are marked by God with the seal of the promised _____ _____, who is the deposit guaranteeing the inheritance of the saints. What do you imagine that inheritance might be?

12. According to 1 Corinthians 6:19,20, at conversion our bodies become a _____ of the Holy Spirit, who is in us. What should this motivate us to do?

13. Read 1 Corinthians 12:13 and complete the following:

   "For we were all baptized by _____ Spirit into _____ body—whether Jews or Greeks, whether slave or free" There is no prejudice or discrimination with God! The presence of His Holy Spirit makes us equal in His eyes! What does that fact mean to you?

THE CONTINUING MINISTRY OF THE HOLY SPIRIT
The Greek word *paraclete,* translated variously as Counselor/ Helper/Comforter, means "the one who comes alongside."

14. Read John 14:16-19,26. What does Jesus promise His followers that the Holy Spirit will do for them?

15. Read 2 Thessalonians 2:13 and complete the following: "From the beginning, God chose you to be _____ through the sanctifying _____ of the Spirit and belief in the _____." Sanctification means being made holy, to become more and more like Jesus in character and attitudes.

   Who does the sanctifying according to this verse?

16. According to Titus 3:3-6, what else does the Holy Spirit do for those who accept His salvation?

17. Read Romans 8:12-17. Verse 16 tells us, "The Spirit himself
    _____ with our spirit that we are God's
    _____."

18. According to Ephesians 1:17, what does the Holy Spirit give us
    when we ask, and what is the purpose of these gifts?

19. According to Ephesians 2:18, the Holy Spirit gives us
    _____ to God.

20. In Ephesians 5:18 and Colossians 3:16, we are commanded to *be
    filled* with the Holy Spirit and let God's Word *dwell* in us. How are
    these two actions related?

21. Read 1 Corinthians 12:1,4-11. This passage describes the gifts of
    the Holy Spirit—special spiritual gifts that are given to believers by
    Him. Every believer has been given at least one spiritual gift. What
    does verse 7 say is the purpose of these spiritual gifts?

22. Read Galatians 5:22,23. What character qualities make up the
    "fruit of the Spirit?"

 Action Step: The "seeds" of the fruit of the Spirit are planted
in our lives when we accept Jesus Christ as our Savior. As we
continually allow the Holy Spirit to work in our lives, these
nine attributes will become more and more evident—"bearing
fruit." Which spiritual fruit do you especially need to nurture
in your life right now?

23. Read John 15:1-17. Although the Holy Spirit is not directly mentioned by name in this passage, His presence is implied in phrases such as "without Me, you can do nothing." What are some of the benefits of abiding, or remaining, in Christ?

    How is this passage related to the fruit of the Spirit in Galatians 5:22,23?

24. Read John 4:23,24. Jesus says if you want to worship God rightly you must worship him in _____ and _____. What does worshiping Him in spirit and in truth mean to you?

EXPERIENCING THE FULLNESS OF THE HOLY SPIRIT

The Lord's Prayer in Matthew 6:9-13 and Luke 11:1-4 is a model prayer Jesus gave to His disciples. In the Luke account Jesus followed the prayer with a story to motivate us to pray and told us what to pray for.

25. What is the point of the story in Luke 11:5-13? What did Jesus say we need to keep on asking, seeking and knocking for?

    What assurance did Jesus give that if we keep asking, seeking and knocking that God will answer by giving the Holy Spirit?

26. Read Romans 8:26. What is the role of the Holy Spirit in prayer and what encouragement does that give you as you learn to pray?

Action Step: If you want to learn more about prayer, begin reading Psalms. As you study the psalms, you will learn that praying involves conversing honestly with God.

THOUGHTS FOR REFLECTION

Apart from the Holy Spirit as depicted in the Bible, the road to spirituality is full of dead ends, traps and deceptions. The Bible clearly teaches that those who worship God must worship Him in Spirit and in truth. This means that it is possible to be deceived by the enemy of our souls, the father of lies, as Jesus called Satan (see John 8:44). The masterful deception of the devil involves drawing humans into worshiping him and causing them to think they are in fact involved with God.

As we have seen, one of the names used to describe the Holy Spirit is *paraclete*, meaning "the one who is alongside us." As a boy growing up in an elementary British boarding school, I looked forward to seeing my parents during visitation hours each Saturday. But because they were about five hours away by train, and because of time, distance, expense and their work schedule, they did not make it to see me every week. The Saturdays they did not show up were very disappointing and lonely for me. Sometimes, I would break down in tears.

Even though I knew deep inside that my parents loved me, I missed their physical presence and personal touch. Not yet having begun a personal relationship with God through Jesus Christ, I was unable to ask Him to fill the void I felt within. It was not until later in life when I became a Christian that I realized that God understood and felt the pain of my inner loneliness and that His Holy Spirit wanted to be with me and comfort me.

CONCLUSION

The Holy Spirit as the Third Person of the Trinity is a real Person with a divine purpose in this world that is fulfilled in our lives as we partner with Him.

His divine power was instrumental in the birth of Jesus Christ (see Luke 1:26-35). It is indispensable for spiritual conversion. He has been sent by God to dwell within us to enable us to know God, receive His wisdom and bear spiritual fruit as we go through this life and live on through eternity.

Every Christian believer is given spiritual gifts and daily power to serve others, to bring the gospel to the whole world and to live a godly life.

CLIMBING HIGHER

A. If Christ has come into your life by faith, and if you have been a regular partaker in Holy Communion (see chapter 2, p. 33), you need to take the step of baptism. There was no ambiguity when Jesus commanded His followers in Matthew 28:18-20 to disciple and to baptize "in the name of the Father and of the Son and of the Holy Spirit."

Throughout the book of Acts which chronicles the growth of the Early Church, conversion was followed by baptism (i.e., Acts 2:38-41; 16:30-33). Baptism is a public witness that represents our death to sin with Christ and our resurrection with Him to newness of life (see Romans 6:3,4). If you have not done so already, talk to your pastor and receive whatever instruction you need before you follow through and take the very important step of being baptized.

B. Ask God to fill you with His Holy Spirit. We have seen that the promise of the Father was that Jesus Christ would baptize believers with the Holy Spirit. Luke 11:9-13 urges us to ask and keep on asking for the Holy Spirit with the confidence that God will answer our prayer because it is obviously His will. The Father is more desirous of giving us the Holy Spirit than we are of asking Him for His wonderful gift.

C. Review this chapter and consider the impact the Holy Spirit has had on your life so far. Where do you especially need the help of the Holy Spirit in your life? Do you need more understanding of His

Word? Ask Him for it! Do you need to develop one particular fruit of the Spirit in your life? Ask Him! Do you need the courage to share Christ with a friend? He promises to empower you; just ask!

— FOUR —
FAITH

KEY VERSE
"Without faith it is impossible to please God, because anyone who comes to him must believe that he exists and that he rewards those who earnestly seek him." Hebrews 11:6

BIG LIES
- You can do anything if you truly believe…in yourself.
- By tuning into the vibrations of the universe, you can overcome anything, including aging or even death.
- Faith is a crutch for the weak.
- It doesn't really matter what you have faith in, so long as it works for you.
- Faith in God leads to intolerance, fanaticism, hatred and bigotry.
- You can only trust what can be proven scientifically.

GOD'S TRUTH
For many religious seekers, the chief interest in spirituality and salvation is not the destination, but the journey and the search. Jesus' promise of eternal life offers both an eternal home for those who believe in the God and Father of our Lord Jesus Christ and a soul-stirring adventure for those who exercise faith in God through the power of the Holy Spirit.

WHAT *Is* FAITH?
Of the three essential Christian virtues—faith, hope and love—faith is mentioned first (see 1 Corinthians 13:13) because it is the first step taken along the Christian's life journey. Biblical faith is not conjuring

up a feeling within yourself that something will happen if you just believe hard enough. Rather, biblical faith has as its focus and theme a trustworthy and good Father God.

1. Reread Hebrews 11:6 (the key verse for this chapter). The first rule of Christian faith is admitting that there is a God—and, incidentally, you're not it! What is the second, according to this verse?

2. "Now faith is the substance of things hoped for, the evidence of things not seen" (Hebrews 11:1, *NKJV*). The word "substance" means "reality or essence." The word "evidence" means "proof or conviction." Based on these definitions, write your own description of faith.

THE FAITH OF JESUS

Jesus Christ is God the Son, but He is also the perfect Son of Man. By studying Jesus' example we can learn something about having a conversational relationship with God and the power of a single phrase uttered in faith.

3. Hebrews 2:17 describes Jesus. Why was Jesus made to be human?

4. Read John 5:17-20. Jesus, the perfect Man, was closer than anyone has ever been to God the Father, yet what did Jesus wait for God to show Him?

5. As you read the following verses, note the powerful words of Jesus and the results of His words.

Jesus' Words	The Results of His Words

Matthew 9:2

Matthew 9:6,7

Matthew 9:22

Matthew 9:29,30

Matthew 15:28

Mark 4:39

What did Jesus demonstrate about the amazing power of the words of faith?

6. Read Mark 6:5,6. What is the result of unbelief?

THE ENERGY OF FAITH

The Bible teaches us that certain things provide energy for our faith. Read 1 Corinthians 10:13 and Philippians 4:13. According to these verses it is *always* possible to believe God and please Him! Therefore, faith is always a choice. There is never a time when you are forced to disobey or to not have faith. You can choose to either believe your circumstances, or to believe God, who is always trustworthy.

7. How might the following examples of difficult circumstances siphon off the energy of your faith?

   Negative circumstances: You've just found out you have a serious illness.

   Doubt: You don't see how God can help you out of a tough financial situation.

   Fear: You fear ridicule if you share Christ with a friend.

8. Read Romans 10:17. What power source mentioned here builds our faith?

   According to 1 Corinthians 12:9,11, who gives the gift of faith?

9. James 2:26 states that our faith is dead without _____.

To energize faith requires action—acting on what we know about God and His trustworthy faithfulness.

10. Read Matthew 14:22-33. Why did Peter begin to sink? What did he begin to focus on rather than on Jesus?

    What action did Peter need to do to keep from sinking?

THE EXERCISE OF FAITH

There are four types of faith. All four types of faith stretch us beyond our natural capacities and boundaries and are anchored in the solid foundation of God's character and promises. Here are some practical steps toward exercising faith in each category.

JUSTIFYING FAITH

This is "life-saving" faith. The basis of our faith is what we believe about Jesus Christ.

11. Read Romans 5:1,2 and complete the following: "Therefore, since we have been _____ through _____, we have peace with God through our Lord Jesus Christ, through whom we have gained access by _____ into this grace in which we now stand."

12. In Genesis 15:6, it says that Abram (Abraham) believed the Lord and it was credited to him as _____.

    In John 14:1 Jesus tells us it is not enough to trust/believe in God; He tells us also to trust/believe in _____. What has Jesus done for us that makes us right with God? How does that prove that God and Jesus can be trusted?

ACTIVE FAITH

An active, growing faith believes what God is teaching us through the Bible and obediently acts on that faith.

13. Read Titus 1:9; 2 Timothy 3:16,17 and Hebrews 4:12. There is no substitute for letting God's Word richly dwell within you. Why is knowing God's Word important to the building of your faith?

Action Step: When in your schedule would be the best time each day for you to read and study the Bible and pray? If you have not already done so, set aside time each day to spend with God. When you read the Bible, ask the Holy Spirit to enlighten your mind and spirit.

14. Read Hebrews 10:24,25. Why do you suppose it is important to the growth of your faith to meet with other Christians?

Action Step: God never intended for you to follow Jesus in isolation from other believers. If you have not already done so, find a church where Jesus Christ is not just an optional way to God, but honored as God—and where the Bible is not just a book bound by time and culture, but honored as the ever relevant truth of God.

15. Read Ephesians 5:19,20. How do you suppose praising and worshiping God contribute to the growth of your faith?

The power of God is released in our lives when we regularly come to Him in praise and worship, both individually and with other believers. The psalms are a great source of material to use in praise and worship.

SANCTIFYING FAITH
This is the faith that dramatically changes our lives.

16. Read Acts 26:18 and complete the following: "Open their eyes and turn them from darkness to light, and from the power of Satan to God, so that they may receive _____ of sins and a place among those who are _____ by _____ in me."

According to 1 Thessalonians 4:1-8, what is God's will for you?

17. According to Matthew 18:3,4 and 1 Peter 5:6, what character quality really pleases God?

What does being humble mean?

18. Read Romans 12:2 and complete the following: Do not _____ any longer to the pattern of this _____, but be _____ by the renewing of your mind. Unfortunately, the biggest problem of the Church is compromising with the culture. How is following Jesus counter to your local culture?

19. Read Philippians 2:13. Who is it that helps us to _____ and to _____ according to God's good purpose?

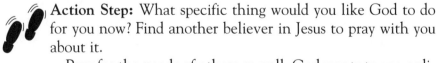 **Action Step:** If you are feeling a lack of desire or zeal to follow Jesus, ask God for more. It is something He wants to give you.

MOUNTAIN-MOVING FAITH

20. Read Matthew 17:20. What is this kind of faith capable of?

Action Step: What specific thing would you like God to do for you now? Find another believer in Jesus to pray with you about it.

Pray for the needs of others as well. God wants to use ordinary believers to bring restoration, healing and God's blessing to others. When others see that God is working through regular people like you, and not just through Pastor Super-Spiritual, they will know it is Jesus who is alive, Jesus who is powerful, and Jesus who answered their prayer!

21. What do each of the following passages teach about faith?

	What I Must Do	What God Will Do
Mark 11:24		
John 14:12-14		
John 15:7,8		
John 15:16		

 Action Step: Read Mark 11:25. Please pause and ask the Holy Spirit to reveal to you anyone against whom you are holding unforgiveness. If you want God to answer your prayers, you need to forgive that person. Now, ask God to show you what to pray for in the name of Jesus. Bring that request to the Father.

THE RESULTS OF FAITH

22. To understand some of the results of faith, read the Scripture verses listed below on the left and draw a line to match them correctly to the result listed in the column on the right side.

a. Matthew 8:16   a blessing for believing,
                                    without seeing

b. John 20:29   deliverance from
                                    demons and disease

c. 1 Thessalonians 1:8-10   deliverance from God's
                                    wrath

d. 1 Timothy 1:5   overcomes the world

e. 1 John 5:4   helps produce love

WHAT ABOUT DISAPPOINTMENT?

There is a significant difference between faith and presuming on God's promises. If we presume we know what God is doing, and He doesn't act according to our expectations, we can be disappointed.

23. As we have seen in the faith of Jesus and the exercise of faith, faith is our response to God's initiative. Have you ever misunderstood what God was doing in a situation in which you prayed for help and thought you didn't receive His help? As you look back at the situation, how did God answer your prayer in a totally unexpected, yet more productive way?

24. Read Romans 10:8-11. Whether our prayers are answered in the way we expect or not, what is the bedrock promise of God to those who call upon His name?

THOUGHTS FOR REFLECTION

Charles Blondin, the tightrope walker, held a crowd of spectators spellbound as he walked a tightrope stretched across Niagara Falls. After making it safely to the other side and responding joyously to the cheers, he threw out a challenge to the group. He asked if the crowd believed that he could cross the falls once again while carrying someone on his shoulders. First one and then another shouted, "I believe!" But when Blondin asked who would be that "someone," no one responded. Finally, his manager, a Mr. McDougle, said he would. McDougle climbed on Blondin's back and was carried safely to the other side.

The lesson for us is this: We need to hear God's Word, believe God's Word and *act* on God's Word. Then when the times come in life and we look down into the deep chasm and feel that our faith is getting wobbly and any slipup can spell disaster, we as believers in Christ need to remember Who is carrying us to the other side.

CONCLUSION

Faith is one of the great virtues of the Christian life, along with hope and love. Faith is essential to pleasing God. A just and fair God provides a measure of faith to help us in our human journey to find Him, and having found Him, to trust Him for the rest of our lives and beyond. Faith is energized by the truth of the Word of God, by fervently believing and acting on God's promises and our strong spiritual commitment to Jesus Christ. The exercise of a living, dynamic faith involves standing on the promises of God, praying for spiritual breakthroughs that only God can give, and trusting God to break through and act in every situation.

CLIMBING HIGHER

A. Write down at least one of the hindrances you are presently experiencing in your walk of faith. What causes you to doubt the promises of God?

Next, prayerfully surrender this hindrance to the Lord in Jesus' name and trust Him to remove it.

B. Confess your faith to God, yourself, your spiritual enemies and others. Each day this coming week, take the time to pray a prayer of confession of your faith that includes the following:

- Confess that Jesus Christ died and rose again (see Romans 10:9,10).
- Confess that you are crucified with Christ (see Galatians 2:20).
- Confess that you are dead to sin and failure (see Romans 6:4).
- Confess that you are utterly free from all sin and condemnation (see Romans 8:1).
- Confess that God has placed you in Christ, has given you His Holy Spirit and that He has made you to produce good fruit (see Ephesians 1:11-14; 2:10).
- Confess that you have victory over the enemy (see 2 Corinthians 10:4,5; 1 John 3:8).
- And finally, confess continually that Jesus Christ is Lord and Master of your life.

C. It is fairly common for certain groups to corrupt and give entirely different meanings to Christian terms. Therefore, you cannot assume people using the same words are talking about the same thing.

For example, in New Age understanding:

- The ascension of Christ describes the realization of the Christ-consciousness in you, that you are divine— instead of Jesus being seated at the right hand of God the Father.
- "At-one-ment" describes complete identification of humans with God—not the *atonement*, which is the cleansing of our sins through the blood of Christ.
- "The kingdom of God is within you" reinterprets Jesus' words to mean that each of us is divine, without having to repent from sins and getting right with God—a denial of the core of Jesus' teaching about God.

— FIVE —

HOPE

KEY VERSES

"Praise be to the God and Father of our Lord Jesus Christ! In his great mercy he has given us new birth into a living hope through the resurrection of Jesus Christ from the dead, and into an inheritance that can never perish, spoil or fade—kept in heaven for you, who through faith are shielded by God's power until the coming of the salvation that is ready to be revealed in the last time." 1 Peter 1:3-5.

BIG LIES

- You create your own heaven and hell.
- If enough people meditate and raise their consciousness, a harmonic convergence will bring peace to earth.
- Everyone eventually goes to heaven—if there is a heaven.
- Self-realization and self-actualization are the most important spiritual goals.
- Image is everything.
- Heaven is just "pie in the sky when you die."

GOD'S TRUTH

God has created us with an insatiable yearning for heaven. In our rebellion against God, we try to fill that longing with many things, putting our trust in false hopes that inevitably disappoint. The only One that can fulfill our longing for heaven is God Himself, who created both heaven and us for Himself. He alone is absolutely trustworthy and our only true hope. What we believe about God and life after death affects how we choose to live in the here and now.

THE PURSUIT OF HOPE

1. Read Proverbs 13:12. Humans desperately need hope. We pour precious resources of money and time into activities that we believe will satisfy us or provide security. Choose two or three of the following things and answer the question: What do people hope to gain from the following activities?

Psychics and astrologers   Crystals, pyramids, chanting
The stock market   The lottery
Psychoanalysts   Cosmetic surgery
Drugs and alcohol   Pornography
Casual sex   Work
Status symbols   Gangs
Bodybuilding   The latest fad or fashion

Which of the above have you ever put your hope in? What has been the result?

Read Matthew 6:19-21,25-27,31-33. What do these verses say about our frantic attempts to gain things?

Read Luke 12:15-21. What would be Jesus' admonition to those who say, "He who dies with the most toys wins"?

2. Read Ecclesiastes 1:2,14. The message of the book of Ecclesiastes is that without God, life is meaningless, like "chasing after the wind." According to the following passages, what human pursuits result in emptiness?

Ecclesiastes 1:16-18

Ecclesiastes 2:1,2

Ecclesiastes 2:17-23

Ecclesiastes 5:10-12

THE HOPE OF JESUS

Jesus' hope was not based on feelings; it was a solid reliance in an all-good, all-powerful God who is in charge of human history and who can be trusted to bring about His good purposes in His best timing.

IN THE GOD OF HISTORY

In the book of Exodus, God heard the groaning of the Israelites who were oppressed in Egypt (see 2:23-25). God answered their prayers by sending Moses, miraculously delivering Israel, giving them a new Law and a place to worship Him. This great deliverance demonstrated God's compassion for people in slavery as well as His absolute supremacy over the gods and rulers of the earth.

3. Read Exodus 15:1-18. How does God, as described in this passage, contrast with the deist's idea that God created the world and then left it to take care of itself?

   How about you? Do you think God is able to intervene in your life? What evidence have you seen of His intervention?

IN THE GOD OF THE AGE TO COME
In the religions of the ancient Near East, time was tied to the seasons of the year and determined by the fertility rituals. The Bible broke this mold and said that human history, as we know it, will end one day; that God's truth, mercy, goodness and justice will eventually win and that evil will be punished.

4. Read Revelation 20:11,12. If the Bible is true, our thoughts and actions can carry eternal consequences. But if things just happen over and over again or if there is nothing at all after death, what does it matter in history what we do?

IN THE FATHER WHO CARES
We can learn a lot about the hope of Jesus from His *knowledge* about what God is like in the Sermon on the Mount (Matthew 5—7).

5. Complete the following statements from Matthew 5 and 6.

5:11,12—God will greatly _____ those who are persecuted because of Him.

5:16—God desires the _____ of His children.

5:18—God will fulfill His _____ which includes His commands *and* His promises.

5:35—God is the Great _____.

5:44,45—God loves even His _____ .
(If God asks us to love our enemies, what does that say about God?)

5:48—God is _____.

6:3,4—God sees what is done in _____ and rewards those who do good.

6:6-8—God knows what you _____ before you ask.

6:14,15—God _____ us if we will _____ others.

6:24—God wants us to make Him our _____, rather than allowing money to be our _____.

6:31-33—God will give us whatever we _____.

IN THE "JOY SET BEFORE HIM."

6. Read Hebrews 12:2,3 and compare it with Hebrews 2:10,14-17. What hope helped Jesus endure the Cross?

THE SCOPE OF OUR HOPE

Christian hope is based in the eternal character and promises of God, revealed most fully in Christ. Christian hope spans the present into the age to come—what happens after death and into eternity.

AN ETERNAL HOME

7. Read John 14:1-6. What did Jesus promise His followers? What images does Jesus use to convey the idea of our eternal life in heaven?

How is Jesus' promise of an eternal home with God different from the belief that there is nothing after death?

How do you feel about Jesus' promise to prepare a place for you in heaven?

Reread 1 Peter 1:3-5 (the key verses). What is the "living hope" of the believer in Christ? Upon what is this hope based?

ETERNAL LIFE HERE AND NOW!

8. According to John 6:47,54, when does a person gain eternal life?

In John 10:10 (*NKJV*), Jesus promised us, "I have come that they may have life, and that they may have it abundantly." Our eternal life begins when we accept Jesus as our Savior and Lord. When we live in fellowship with God, we will experience life on this earth "to the full" (*NIV*).

9. Read Colossians 1:26-28. What a magnificent promise we find in these verses! The mystery, hidden in the past but now revealed in the saints (the ones who believe in Jesus), is that _____ is in you, and that He is your "_____ of _____" (v. 27); that is, the promise of heaven, the process of being perfected in Christ, and being able to glorify God even now.

A NEW SPIRITUAL POSITION
According to Romans 6:4-6 and Ephesians 2:4-6, we who believe in Christ are right now identified spiritually with Christ's death, resurrection and ascension to heaven!

10. What implications might each of the following facts about your new position have in your life?

You have died to sin with Christ.

You have been resurrected with Christ to new life.

You have been raised with Christ to the very throne of God.

UNDERSTANDING SUFFERING

11. When we have been justified—made right with God—by faith, according to Romans 5:1-5, what difference does it make when we go through suffering? Why can we actually rejoice when going through suffering?

What is the four-step process that ends in hope?

What will never happen if we are firmly anchored in Christian hope?

NO CONDEMNATION

12. Read Romans 7:21-25 and 8:1. We struggle to do what is right and often fail. For those who struggle against sin, how important is the promise that there is "no condemnation" if we are "in Christ Jesus"?

THE ENABLEMENT OF THE HOLY SPIRIT

13. Read Romans 8:1,2,9. How can we ever please God?

   What does it mean to live according to the Spirit?

THE RESURRECTION OF THE BODY
The Bible clearly teaches that in heaven, believers will have resurrected bodies. This belief affirms the goodness of God's original material creation and goes against all mysticisms that teach that "the spirit" is good and the material world itself is evil.

14. Read the following verses and complete the statements:

   John 5:25-29—Jesus made the astounding claim that at His voice those who hear His voice will _____ (v. 25).

   John 11:25—Just before raising Lazarus from the dead, Jesus claimed, "I am the resurrection and the life. He who...lives and _____ in me will never _____."

   1 Corinthians 15:51-57—The conclusion to a whole chapter on the resurrection says that through Christ, believers will have victory over _____ (see vv. 54,55).

   2 Corinthians 5:5-10—The Holy Spirit is the guarantee of _____.

   How does the Bible's teaching on resurrection of the body contrast with the doctrine of reincarnation? (See pp. 110-111.)

GOD'S PROVISION FOR HIS CHILDREN

15. According to Romans 8:26,27, what is one ministry of the Holy Spirit?

    In Romans 8:28, what very significant promise is made to those who love God and are called according to His purpose? What hope does this promise give you?

16. Read Romans 8:31-39. Are there any forces arrayed against the believer in Jesus Christ that will eventually win? Can anyone condemn us? Can any evil spirit separate us from God's love? What does this passage do for your hope monitor?

THE NEW HEAVEN AND THE NEW EARTH
In the Bible, "heaven" and "the new heaven and the new earth" both describe the glorious promises of God to His people (see 2 Peter 3:13).

17. Read Romans 8:17,18. According to this passage, we are "heirs of God" and "co-heirs with Christ." If we share in His suffering, we will also share in His _____.

    According to the Bible, our purpose is to worship God. Creation was made by God to help us worship Him. What does Romans 8:19-21 say that both creation and our own bodies are yearning for?

    Read 2 Peter 3:13. What phrase here expresses the same eager expectation seen in the Romans 8:19-21 passage?

18. Match the concept on the left to the correct Scripture reference on the right.

The following will cease to exist in the new heaven and the new earth:

a. Tears, death, crying, pain   Romans 8:38,39

b. Sickness   Revelation 7:16

c. The devil   Revelation 10:6

d. Hunger and thirst   Revelation 20:10

e. Time as we know it   Revelation 21:3,4

f. Sinners   Revelation 21:8

g. Separation from God   Revelation 22:2

19. Read Revelation 21:1-7,22-27 and 22:1-5, then list those things that you will look forward to in heaven.

THE GOOD NEWS

20. What does 1 Peter 3:15 advise us to do?

How can you be better prepared to share the gospel with others?

21. Read Matthew 28:18-20. What command does Jesus give His disciples? How wide is the scope of their mission?

22. Read Revelation 7:9,10. At the end of history, it is certain that people from every tribe and tongue and ethnic group will be represented worshiping the Lamb—Jesus Christ—in the throne room of heaven. What do God's people need to do now in order to advance God's purpose to bring the message of Jesus Christ to the whole world?

OUR BLESSED HOPE

23. Read Titus 2:13. The Christian's "blessed hope" is the "appearing," or the Second Coming of Jesus Christ when history as we know it will end and a new heaven and a new earth replaces them. How does it make you feel to know that Christ will return someday, perhaps in the near future?

    Read 1 John 3:2,3. What will the children of God finally see and what will that vision do to them?

HOPE: THE ENERGY OF PRAYER

A spiritual dynamic is released when we open our inner lives—heart, mind and spirit—to Christian hope and allow God's Spirit to reveal what to pray for.

24. In Ephesians 1:17-19, Paul prayed that the Spirit of revelation and wisdom might come upon the Ephesians and _____ the eyes of their hearts concerning their true hope, riches and power of God in their lives.

25. Read Matthew 6:9-13. This model prayer which the Lord Jesus taught His disciples contains seven requests, each one based upon certain hopes about God. What is the hope behind each request?

Holy is Your name

Your kingdom come

Your will be done on earth as it is in heaven

Give us today our daily bread

Forgive us our debts [sins], as we also have forgiven our debtors [those who sin against us]

Lead us not into temptation

Deliver us from the evil one

26. Read Hebrews 6:18. Christian hope does not come to us by osmosis and is not forced upon us. We are called of our own free will to reach out and take _____ of the _____.

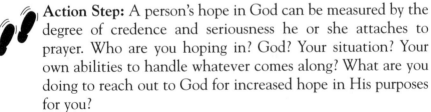 **Action Step:** A person's hope in God can be measured by the degree of credence and seriousness he or she attaches to prayer. Who are you hoping in? God? Your situation? Your own abilities to handle whatever comes along? What are you doing to reach out to God for increased hope in His purposes for you?

THOUGHTS FOR REFLECTION

Harry Houdini earned the reputation of being a legendary magician several decades ago. He became very well known for his ability to pick any lock with ease and get himself out of a box or cage. Once a group asked him to take up the challenge of a specially locked cell they had prepared for him. After he got in the cell, a crowd watched on the edge of their seats to see if he would get out. Houdini fiddled with the lock and gave up unsuccessfully after two hours. In exhaustion from the trauma of his struggle, he fell down. As he fell, he hit the door and it opened. He had been tricked. Though the lock seemed tightly secured, the door was actually easy to open with the slightest pressure.

In the midst of our most difficult trials we may seem hopelessly boxed in. However, our hope in Christ encourages us to hang in there; God will open a door for us.

CONCLUSION

When we have biblical hope, it energizes us to live in a manner that will prepare us for our future in heaven promised by God. The hope God provides must be cultivated in the midst of life's adverse circumstances. We must never forget that this world is not our home (see Philippians 3:20). Our souls will ultimately live on either in heaven or in hell. The Christian hope is enhanced by God's promise that the things we consider as plagues in this present life will cease to exist in heaven. In place of suffering and evil will be a perfection of everlasting love, joy and peace in God's presence. We will be an integral part of God's divine mission for eternity.

CLIMBING HIGHER

A. Look over the list in question 18 (p. 68) of things that will cease to exist in heaven. Write down three things that have plagued your life. Now in hope, offer up a prayer of thanksgiving that someday you will be in heaven with the Lord Himself, freed from these earthly challenges.

B. Reread the list of the characteristics of heaven in questions 18 and 19 (p. 68). Tell God how thankful you are for His promises of heaven and what items you are specifically looking forward to enjoying in heaven.

C. Do you know someone who needs the hope of Jesus in his or her life? Pray for that person and for an opportunity to share the Good News with him or her. Remember to ask for the Holy Spirit's empowerment to share God's Word.

~ SIX ~

LOVE

KEY VERSES

"But the goal of our instruction is love from a pure heart and a good conscience and a sincere faith." 1 Timothy 1:5 (*NASB*)

"And now abide faith, hope, love, these three; but the greatest of these is love." 1 Corinthians 13:13 (*NKJV*)

BIG LIES

- Love is an overpowering feeling; it may come and go.
- You need to love yourself before you can love anyone else.
- Love can only be found in your soul mate.
- Psychic hotlines are a good source of information on love.
- Your body belongs to you so you can do whatever you want with it.
- Love is just the interaction of chemicals and hormones in the body.

GOD'S TRUTH

Only if we know the purpose for which we were created can
  we be truly wise.
What is our purpose? To worship God.
How do we worship God? Through faith, hope and love.
We begin by faith, and will be made perfect by sight.
Faith believes in God; hope and love pray to God.
We do not see what we believe nor what we hope for.
Without love, faith profits nothing.
Without love, hope cannot exist.
Without faith, there can be neither hope nor love.
Ultimately, what counts is faith expressing itself through love.

—St. Augustine[1]

THE GOAL OF BIBLICAL TEACHING

In our culture the word "love" is most often identified with romantic or sexual love. The New Testament's primary use of the word "love," however, refers to brotherly love and God's love.

1. Reread 1 Timothy 1:5 (see the key verse). The goal of Christian instruction is love from a _____ heart, a _____ conscience and a _____ faith. Why are each of these attributes important in showing love?

THE LOVE OF JESUS

In the Bible, love begins *within* God, not just *with* God. From eternity past to the ageless future, the one God who has always existed as Father, Son and Holy Spirit has always dwelt in perfect harmony and true, unselfish abiding love.

FOR THE FATHER

2. What do you learn about the relationship between God the Father and God the Son in Mark 1:11 and 14:32-36?

   Throughout His life on earth, Jesus perfectly loved God and submitted to His Father's will. Read Mark 14:32-36, which takes place in the Garden of Gethsemane on the eve of Jesus' crucifixion. According to Mark 14:36, how does Jesus address God and what does that tell you about His relationship with God the Father? What was the conversation between the Father and the Son about? How was it resolved?

   Read John 14:26 and 15:26. According to these verses, who sends the Holy Spirit? What does the Holy Spirit do?

Among the equal Persons of the Trinity, God the Father loves God the Son; God the Son loves and is obedient to God the Father's will; God the Holy Spirit loves and subordinates Himself to both God the Father and God the Son. There are no jealousies or rivalries within the Trinity; rather there is an eternal expression of perfect love.

FOR HIS PEOPLE
Chapters 13 through 17 in the Gospel of John contain Jesus' last teachings for His disciples on the eve of His crucifixion.

3. How does John 13:1 describe Jesus' love for His followers? How has Jesus demonstrated His love for you?

The entire chapter of John 17 is Jesus' fervent prayer for His disciples and those who would come to believe in His name through the disciples. What is His final request in John 17:26?

THE LOVE OF JESUS—IN US!
Jesus wants His followers to be filled with His and the Father's love. Following Jesus means letting the love of Christ animate us and work through us.

4. Read Matthew 22:37-39. Jesus Christ was the perfect embodiment of His teaching. What is the basis of these two great commandments?

GROUNDED IN GOD'S TRUTH
The book of 1 John could be considered a love letter from Jesus Christ to us through the pen of His disciple John. The fourth chapter is a profound statement explaining the Triune (meaning "three-in-one") God's love for us and our love for God.

5. Read 1 John 4:7-12. God took the initiative to love us first. What was God's motivation in sending Jesus (v. 9)?

What was the mission or intended purpose of God's action (v. 10)?

What is the sign that God lives in us (v. 12)?

6. Read 1 John 4:13-18. What tests does John give to determine whether we have the Holy Spirit living in us? In what ways do we "acknowledge that Jesus is the Son of God" (vv. 15,16)?

7. Read 1 John 4:19-21. Why do you suppose a person who says, "I love God" yet hates another brother or sister in Christ is called a liar?

A SUPERNATURAL GIFT
We don't manufacture this love on our own power—it is a gift from God.

8. Until we accept Christ as Lord and Savior of our lives, we are separated from Christ and "without hope and without God in the world" (Ephesians 2:1,12). How close can we come to loving like God wants us to love in this separated condition?

Read Ephesians 2:4-10. We can't ever earn God's love with our "good works," but according to verse 4, why did God make us alive in Christ?

9. According to John 15:1-5, what are the conditions for bearing fruit? What kind of fruit do you suppose Christ is speaking of here?

 Action Step: How can you be better connected to Jesus, the True Vine (see John 15:1), the source of the believer's spiritual life and power to produce fruit?

THE NEW COMMANDMENT

10. Read John 13:34,35. This is the most amazing commandment Jesus gave. He called this the _____ _____. What was so new about it?

Jesus was actually *commanding* His disciples to love one another as *He* had loved them! How could this be possible? What would Jesus and God need to give the disciples for them to come anywhere near to fulfilling this commandment? (See John 14:26 and 15:26.)

According to John 13:35, what would be the result of this kind of love; what would convince people that believers are disciples of Jesus? What evidence of this type of love have you seen among Christians?

On the other hand, what kind of example is it when Christians do what comes naturally: take advantage of each other, oppress each other, take each other to court, or even injure or kill one another?

Why do we need supernatural help of the Holy Spirit to love with Christ's own love?

A DECISION OF THE WILL

11. People often think of love as a warm, fuzzy feeling. If they "feel" loving, then they act loving; if they do not "feel" loving, then they suppose they are no longer required to act in loving ways. How does the belief that "love is a feeling" damage relationships?

We have seen that Jesus wants His followers to love even their enemies (see Matthew 5:44-48), yet we sometimes find it difficult to love even those closest to us. Why did Jesus command His followers to love even their enemies?

God's way of love requires us to impose a decision to obey God's will rather than following our own will. We have to firmly decide that we will obey God, no matter what our feelings are, then trust God for His supernatural enablement through Christ.

 Action Step: Is there someone that comes to your mind right now toward whom—as an act of your will and trusting in God's enablement—you need to show forgiveness and start practicing God's love? You cannot do this by your own power; you must prayerfully rely on God to make this change in your heart.

LOVE TRANSFORMS ALL OUR RELATIONSHIPS

When we accept the transforming power of God's love, all of our relationships change, beginning with God, extending to our closest circle of family and friends, to those within our own culture and even to other peoples and cultures.

THE SOURCE

12. According to 1 Peter 1:22, how does the Holy Spirit energize believers to express God's love?

A NEW FAMILY

13. Draw a line from the Bible reference to the new relationship we have as believers in Christ.

    a. John 1:12   Jesus is not ashamed to be
                                          called your "brother."

    b. Romans 8:17   You are a member of the great
                                          household of God.

    c. Ephesians 2:16   You are a child of God.

    d. Ephesians 2:19   You are an heir of God and
                                          coheir with Christ.

    e. Hebrews 2:11   You are reconciled with God.

14. As a result of receiving and reflecting the love of God in God's family, relationship dynamics are radically different:

    1 Peter 2:17—Other believers are now your _____ and _____ in Christ.

    Revelation 7:9—You have become part of the family God has been building through the ages, a people from every _____, _____ and language.

TESTS OF LOVE

Following Jesus' way of love means resisting the pressure to conform to the culture, being transformed by the renewing of your mind (see Romans 12:1,2).

HONOR GOD WITH YOUR BODY

The prevailing attitude in our culture regarding sexuality is that your body is your own and you have the right to do with it whatever you want.

15. How does 1 Corinthians 6:18-20 compare with the prevailing cultural attitudes about sexuality?

Do you think it is possible for followers of Jesus who call Him Lord to be different in this area? What promise does Philippians 4:13 give to believers who struggle with *any* deeply engrained sin?

 Action Step: In your present situation—whether single or married—What is your understanding of God's definition of sexual purity? If you are falling short in this area, be honest! Confess it to God and ask Him to help you begin the process of restoration of your sexuality so you can use that gift to glorify Him.

DO NOT LOVE THE WORLD

16. In 1 John 2:15-17, what does John say about the person who loves the world? "The world" in John's writings refers to the cultural system that is in rebellion against God.

What are examples of the cravings of our sinful nature, the lust of our eyes or sinful boasting?

John is saying that some things are eternal and some things simply don't last. What is John's conclusion about the permanence of the world and its desires?

ACCEPT THE FATHER'S DISCIPLINE

17. Read Hebrews 12:1-11. Why do you think God's discipline is so necessary in our lives? What is God's motive when He disciplines us?

   In 1 Corinthians 9:24-27 and Philippians 3:12-14, Paul compares the Christian life to an athlete's training and motivation. What must an athlete do to prepare for the Olympics? How might that compare to a Christian's preparation? What is the prize that believers receive?

SHARE THE GOSPEL

18. Read 2 Timothy 4:2. Who is responsible for telling others about Jesus? Is it the responsibility just of preachers and Christian teachers or "super-Christians," or is it a responsibility for all believers?

Both Paul, the author of 1 and 2 Timothy and much of the New Testament, and Peter, the author of 1 and 2 Peter, as well as many of the early Christians were martyred for following Jesus. While martyrdom for Christ may be rare in North America, in other parts of the world there are believers who love Jesus so much they are willingly dying for Him.

   Read Acts 1:8. What has God promised to give us to empower us to take His message of salvation to others?

 Action Step: How do you feel about telling others about Jesus? What has Christ done for you that would impel you to share Him with others? What are you willing to risk for Him who gave everything for you?

IDENTIFY WITH JESUS

19. Read John 15:18-27. What does Jesus tell His followers to expect and why will this occur?

20. Read Revelation 12:9-11. This passage describes the defeat of Satan. How will Satan be overcome? What were these believers willing to do in order to overcome Satan?

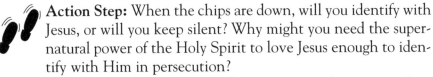 **Action Step:** When the chips are down, will you identify with Jesus, or will you keep silent? Why might you need the super-natural power of the Holy Spirit to love Jesus enough to iden-tify with Him in persecution?

Even though you may not know anyone who is even close to being martyred for their faith in Jesus, could you please pray right now for Christians who might be facing persecution or even death right now in Africa, Asia, Eastern Europe or the former Soviet Union?

IDENTIFY WITH THE LOST

21. Read Matthew 5:13-16. How can God's people be salt and light to those who are far from God without appearing "holier than thou"?

22. In Luke 19:10, Jesus said His mission was to _____and to _____ the lost. The "lost" means those who are far away from God, on the road to hell. If you are one of God's peo-ple, in what ways might God be calling you to identify with "the lost" in order to pray with understanding for their condition?

FOLLOW JESUS WHOLEHEARTEDLY

23. Read Mark 8:34-38. What things does Jesus say we must do if we are to follow Him?

Jesus says that one way or the other, you're going to lose your life. It's your choice: You can waste it on yourself, gaining the whole world yet losing your soul. Or you can lose your life for the sake of Jesus and the gospel and gain everything He has promised to believers.

 Action Step: Ask the Lord if there is anything that you love more than Jesus and His Word. Consider the damage it does to you and others spiritually when you love these things more than God. Confess these things to the Lord now, and ask Him to help you follow and love Him with your whole heart, and to love your neighbor as yourself.

THOUGHTS FOR REFLECTION

Mother Teresa was world renowned for founding the Missionaries of Charity and her work with the poorest of the poor in Calcutta, India. She earned the respect of people of all religions. Yet despite her decades of selfless service, some Christians have questioned whether Mother Teresa believed in salvation by works or focused exclusively on the physical needs of people to the exclusion of their spiritual needs.

It is a myth that Mother Teresa was and the Missionaries of Charity are unconcerned with evangelism. When they are meeting the physical needs of people, they talk about Jesus! As they are cleansing the wounds of a leper or someone who is about to die, they say things such as, "Do you want to know that your prayers will get through to God? Then ask Jesus to help you." "Do you want to meet God with a clean heart? Pray for forgiveness through Jesus." "Do you want to go to heaven? Jesus is your sure way to heaven." "Do you need hope? Jesus is here right now." Mother Teresa and the Missionaries of Charity have never denied that people, no matter their religious background, need Christ.

When questioned about trying to convert other people (a very touchy subject in India), Mother Teresa's answer was always the same. She respected the right of every individual to believe in his or her own religion, but she made it clear that everything that she did was for the love of the Lord Jesus Christ. She clothed the naked, fed the hungry and lifted the dregs of society from the black hole of Calcutta with the power and the love of the Lord Jesus Christ.

CONCLUSION

Erroneous views of love distance us from God and others, directing our lives down the path of despair and eventual disillusion. So how can we begin to understand authentic love?

A healthy view of love begins with the God of the Bible who *is* love. It is the love that we were all created for—to freely receive and to freely give. It elevates our quality of inner life and enables us to touch people around us in an edifying way. It is the love that transforms us into who we were created to be and allows us to experience true intimacy with God and with one another.

Becoming part of God's family involves both accepting His love in accordance with John 3:16 and obedience to the two great commandments (see Matthew 22:37-39). God's love is energized in us as we seek intimacy with Him. God's love grows in us as a result of the work of the Holy Spirit.

Christian love requires Christlike action, demonstrating that His love has conquered our lives. Because He has loved us, we love Him and we obey Him. When Christians surrender to the command to love one another, they create a platform to share a credible and effective witness to a world waiting for God's love to touch them.

CLIMBING HIGHER

A. Write down a negative behavior pattern described in 1 Corinthians 13:4-7 that you presently see in your own life. Confess this to the Lord in prayer, ask for His forgiveness and ask the Holy Spirit to fill you with the love of God.

B. Write down one positive expression of Christian love listed in 1 Corinthians 13:4-7 that you desire to cultivate in your life. Each day this week, ask God to fill you with His Holy Spirit to help you to specifically demonstrate this quality.

C. Starting with your own family, make a list of people around you who have needs. Next, prayerfully ask God to help you express His love in a practical way to each of these people this week. For example, even if you have limited material resources, you can pray and encourage another person just by taking the time to fellowship with them.

 Action Step: To courageously acknowledge Jesus as Lord requires love. Have you ever been ashamed to do so? If so, you were loving the wrong things. Confess that sin to God now, and ask God to help you live...

- as if Jesus were coming with His Father's glory and the holy angels any day now.
- as if you are the bride and Christ is the Bridegroom, and the wedding is any day now.
- boldly as one whose love for Jesus is the most important thing in life.

AND FINALLY...

PERSEVERE in your Christian life. Scripture is clear that we are involved in a spiritual battle. The Christian who endures till the end will be saved for time and eternity.

PREPARE yourself continually. Take another Bible class. You need to be continually studying God's Word and sharing your faith.

PRAY. The prayerless Christian is the powerless Christian. Prayer will bring God's presence, perspective, power, plan and prosperity to your life!

Note:
1. Adapted from St. Augustine's *Enchiridion* (Washington, D. C.: Regnery Publishing, Inc., 1961, 1966) from "Faith, Hope and Love," sections ii-viii. Also see Galatians 5:6.

LEADER'S GUIDE

INTRODUCTION

This leader's guide provides tips on how to lead a seekers' or new believers' class, as well as group activities, discussion and interaction ideas to reinforce each lesson in an interesting way.

PURPOSE OF THIS STUDY

This course is designed for seekers, new believers and Christians who have never taken a starter course on the Christian life. It is ideal for use during the adult Sunday School hour or during a midweek small group study. Each session is designed for 60- to 90-minute meeting times.

PURPOSE OF GROUP DISCUSSION

The purpose of group discussion is to create an open forum for a healthy teacher-guided discussion with the definite intent of reinforcing the learning of biblical truth.

HOW TO LEAD A SMALL GROUP

- Be well prepared.
- Answer the questions ahead of time and be prepared to handle the difficult or controversial questions.
- Allow the class members to express their views. This helps you as the teacher to know where they are spiritually and enables you to lead them in the right direction.
- If you find one person trying to dominate the group, say something like, "I know some of those we have not heard from have something to contribute as well, so please feel free to speak up." Or specifically call on another person to share his or her answer.
- If someone requires more time and attention, say something like, "I would love to set aside some time and discuss that further with you." Then continue on with the lesson. After class, follow up on continuing the discussion with those who are interested.

- Be sensitive to the Holy Spirit. If the Holy Spirit is leading you to spend more time on some points and less on others, follow His leading.
- As a courtesy and in the best interests of all in the class, stick to the lesson outline, so there is measurable progress.
- Problem students that sidetrack the teaching process should be dealt with privately. Consult with the person in charge of Christian education in your church or the pastor if you need additional advice.
- Above all, acknowledge your dependency on God and pray for the Holy Spirit to give you wisdom and be in control of the class.

HINTS FOR LEADERS

T = Trust God. He will help you as you fulfill His Great Commission to teach the Word.

E = Educate yourself so you are well prepared. When you do not know the answer, commit to searching Scripture and consulting other leadership until you find it.

A = Awareness of the culture—live with enough knowledge of the "real" world so your teaching can be relevant to where people are at.

C = Clarity—always strive to be clear in your presentation, using illustrations as needed and being willing to discuss a point until it is clear.

H = Honor—always honor God, His Word and the people you are teaching. An atmosphere of love and a healthy respect for differing viewpoints is vital in fostering an atmosphere for spiritual maturity and growth.

PREPARATION STEPS FOR EACH LESSON
The following are steps that need to be taken before each teaching time:

MATERIALS NEEDED
- An overhead projector and transparency, or white board or chalkboard and pens or chalk
- Identical Bible versions for those who do not have their own
- Pens or pencils

PREPARATION

- Read through and answer the study questions before class.
- Note any questions, concepts or statements that might be difficult or controversial for any of the group members.
- Mark those questions and verses that are the most important ones to cover in case you run short on time before you complete the questions.

God the Father

Preparation
❑ Follow the "Preparation Steps for Each Lesson" (p. 89).
❑ If you are doing Introduction Activity Option 1, you'll need to collect examples of the Big Lies from various media sources.

Warm-Up (10 Minutes)
Introduce yourself and play a simple, nonthreatening get-acquainted game. Ask group members to find someone that was born in the same season—winter, spring, summer or fall. Ask them to learn something else that they have in common with that person. After a minute or two ask the pairs to introduce their partners to the rest of the group.

Note: If you have an odd number of people in a given season, pair up the extra person with someone from another season or make a threesome within that season.

Introduction (10 Minutes)
Choose one of the following activities to introduce the topic.

Activity Option 1
Before class, collect examples of the Big Lies statements from newspapers, magazines, TV, commercials, etc. The visual aids will help stimulate discussion. Ask members to discuss what the various visuals are saying about God.

Activity Option 2
Ask the group members to share the most recent thing they heard someone say about God. Be aware: You may get some blasphemous or shocking responses. Here are some sample responses:

Jesus' name used in vain.
God is a crutch.
Jesus is not the only way to God.

Be prepared to respond biblically, clearly and non-defensively to such viewpoints.

GOD'S TRUTH (30–60 MINUTES)

If your group has members that are unfamiliar with the Bible, give a short lesson on how to find verses in the Bible.

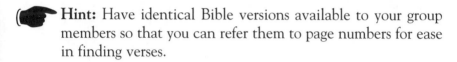 **Hint:** Have identical Bible versions available to your group members so that you can refer them to page numbers for ease in finding verses.

- As you work your way through the lesson, assign verses to be read aloud by volunteers. Work through the lesson question by question.
- Clarify the difference between the powers of spiritual darkness and spiritual light. Reiterate that biblically there is no such thing as the "third force"—a theme common to many current movies—a supernatural force that is neither good nor evil. Explain that there are two opposing and unequal supernatural powers—God and Satan. God is always more powerful than Satan and it is Satan who loses in the end.

CONCLUDING ACTIVITY (10 MINUTES)

To conclude the session, divide the members into groups of three or four and ask them to discuss the following questions. Write the questions on the board or an overhead transparency.

1. What does idolatry mean to you?

2. What are some modern examples of things people idolize instead of God?

3. Suppose you are a "pillar of the community"—a good citizen—and you have an identical twin who is the exact opposite. Your twin goes around your community doing terrible things and identifying him- or herself by your name. For example: You are a municipal court judge and your "evil twin" is arrested for driving under the influence. Your name is splashed all over the newspaper the next morning as being arrested for DUI. How would that make you feel? What would be the ramifications to your private and public life? Relate that to how we, who are created in God's image, treat Him.

- Pray together asking God to reveal Himself to each of the class members.

   Note to Leader: Appendix B: "The Problem with the Goddess" (p. 108) deals with why God is primarily referred to as our Father, rather than as our Mother. Use this material if you have class members who have questions concerning this issue.

SUPPLEMENTAL ACTIVITY

PURPOSE
To be used at the beginning of the first session to help those who are unfamiliar with the Bible to become more familiar.

PREPARATION
- Make an overhead transparency of the reproducible handout Appendix A: "How the Bible Is Arranged" (p. 107).
- **Or** refer group members to page 107 to follow along as you guide them.
- After explaining the chart, assign a verse or two from each section that group members can practice looking up. Suggestions are:

   Old Testament
   Law: Genesis 1:3; Numbers 6:22-27
   History: 1 Samuel 8:4-9
   Poetry: Psalm 19

Major Prophets: Jeremiah 32:17-19
Minor Prophets: Zephaniah 3:17

New Testament
Gospels: Matthew 5:1-12; John 17:20-26
History: Acts 1:4
Epistles of Paul: Ephesians 3:14-21
Epistles of Others: 1 John 2:15-17
Prophecy: Revelation 1:7,8,12-16

- Ask group members to read the verses they find.
- Close in prayer.

GOD THE SON, JESUS CHRIST

PREPARATION
❑ Follow the "Preparation Steps for Each Lesson" (p. 89).
❑ If you are doing Introduction Activity Option 1, you'll need to collect newspaper articles, TV reports or other readings that refer to Jesus Christ or His teachings.

WARM-UP (10 MINUTES)
Ask each class member to briefly share how he or she was lead into his or her life work or profession.

INTRODUCTION (10 MINUTES)
Choose one of the following activities to introduce the topic.

ACTIVITY OPTION 1
Share information from news articles, reports or your own reading that directly or indirectly refer to Jesus Christ or His teachings.

ACTIVITY OPTION 2
Ask any volunteers in the group to share what they have heard or read about what people believe about Jesus.

GOD'S TRUTH (30–60 MINUTES)
• As you work your way through the lesson, assign verses to be read aloud by volunteers. Work through the lesson question by question.
• Clarify the deity and humanity of Jesus Christ.

CONCLUDING ACTIVITY (10 MINUTES)
• Divide the class into small groups of three or four each.
• Write on the board or overhead several false views about who Jesus is.

- Assign one view to each group if possible.
- Ask the groups to discuss how someone could biblically, logically and lovingly approach a person who held such a view, to persuade them about the uniqueness of Jesus Christ.
- Close in prayer.

SUPPLEMENTAL ACTIVITY

- Ask group members to turn to appendix C: "Other Titles and Names for Jesus Christ" (p. 109) in their study guides or make an overhead transparency of the page to display for the whole group.
- Ask for volunteers to read the Scripture passages, then discuss the following:

1. Which of all the names or titles of Jesus is most surprising to you and why?

2. Which one is most meaningful to you and why?

- Challenge group members to take the Action Step.

Note to Leader: Appendix D: "The Problem with Reincarnation" (pp. 110-111) deals with the differences between these opposing beliefs. Use this material if you have class members who have questions concerning this issue.

God the Holy Spirit

Preparation
❑ Follow the "Preparation Steps for Each Lesson" (p. 89).
❑ If you are doing Introduction Activity Option 1, you'll need to find an example of supernatural power from the media.

Warm-Up (10 Minutes)
Ask class members to briefly share about their relationship to a person who has meant a lot to them, such as a child, spouse, parent or close friend.

Introduction (10 Minutes)
Choose one of the following activities to introduce the topic.

Activity Option 1
Share from your reading, an article or TV news report about an example of supernatural power. Most weekend papers report on religious activities in your area. Have the class react to the report biblically.

Activity Option 2
Ask volunteers in the class to share who they think the Holy Spirit is and what exactly He does.

God's Truth (30–60 Minutes)
- As you work your way through the lesson, assign verses to be read aloud by volunteers. Work through the lesson question by question.
- Be prepared to clarify the teaching on the Trinity.

Concluding Activity (10 Minutes)
- Share with the class your answer to the following question: How have you experienced the power of the Holy Spirit?

- Discuss:
  How can you discern whether you are experiencing the presence of the Holy Spirit, your own feelings or the powers of darkness?
- Close in prayer.

Supplemental Activity

Thought Questions on the Trinity
Discuss the following:

1. How might the diversity yet unity of persons within the Trinity encourage parents to allow children to develop their own individual interests, without fearing the unity of the family will be damaged?

2. How might the unity and diversity in the Trinity be more fully reflected by churches in which many racial or ethnic backgrounds are worshiping the one Lord Jesus Christ together?

FAITH

PREPARATION

❑ Follow the "Preparation Steps for Each Lesson" (p. 89).

❑ If you are doing Introduction Activity Option 1, you'll need to find examples from your reading of people who have overcome great difficulties.

WARM-UP (10 MINUTES)

Ask volunteers in the class to share a spiritual experience from their childhood that contributed to or encouraged them in their faith.

INTRODUCTION (10 MINUTES)

Choose one of the following activities to introduce the topic.

ACTIVITY OPTION 1

From articles, news reports or your own reading, share examples of people who, despite impossible odds, have overcome great difficulties. Then emphasize how much more significant is the blessing of faith in God, rather than just positive thinking to make it through a tough time.

ACTIVITY OPTION 2

Ask volunteers to share examples of people they know who have overcome difficult circumstances. Ask them to tell why they think these people were overcomers.

GOD'S TRUTH (30–60 MINUTES)

• As you work your way through the lesson, assign verses to be read aloud by volunteers. Work through the lesson question by question.

• Be prepared to discuss false concepts about faith, such as:

  • Having blind faith, rather than a knowledgeable faith in our trustworthy God;

- Believing that God is obligated to make you wealthy;
- Prove God to me before I believe.

CONCLUDING ACTIVITY (10 MINUTES)

- Plan in advance to have selected people in the class share a testimony of how they placed their faith in God for a specific need and God answered their prayers.
- Close in prayer.

   Note to Leader: Appendix E: "Worldviews As Faith Systems" (pp. 112-113) deals with how people develop a belief system out of their personal worldviews. Use this material if you have class members who have questions concerning this issue.

HOPE

PREPARATION
❏ Follow the "Preparation Steps for Each Lesson" (p. 89).
❏ If you are doing Introduction Activity Option 1, have extra sheets of paper available.

WARM-UP (10 MINUTES)
From your reading or a news report share cultural views about death, afterlife, heaven and hell. Then lead a discussion, asking the class to biblically respond to the views expressed.

INTRODUCTION (10 MINUTES)
Choose one of the following activities to introduce the topic.

ACTIVITY OPTION 1
Give each group member a sheet of paper. Ask members to write down two or three good reasons why they have hope for the future. Then ask each one to share with the group what is on his or her list.

ACTIVITY OPTION 2
Ask volunteers to share how hope was injected into their hearts in the middle of a difficult situation.

GOD'S TRUTH (30–60 MINUTES)
• As you work your way through the lesson, assign verses to be read aloud by volunteers. Work through the lesson question by question.
• Be prepared to share some pointers with the class on what to say to a person who has lost hope in a situation.

CONCLUDING ACTIVITY (10 MINUTES)

- Divide class members into small groups. Based on the lesson, have each group discuss a list of things that all Christians can expect after death. Then have each small group leader share the list with the whole group.
- Have the small groups pray together that any bondage to fear of the future will be broken.
- Close in prayer for the whole group.

SUPPLEMENTAL ACTIVITY

- Ask group members to turn to appendix F: "Hope Fulfilled" (p. 114) in their study guides or make an overhead transparency of the page to display for the whole group.
- Discuss how Jesus was the fulfillment/completion of many things that were written in the Old Testament.

– Leader's Guide for Chapter Six –

LOVE

Preparation
❑ Follow the "Preparation Steps for Each Lesson" (p. 89).

Warm-Up (10 Minutes)
Have each class member share one spiritual goal or desire they want to attain in expressing their love to God and others. Ask them to be specific.

Introduction (10 Minutes)
Choose one of the following activities to introduce the topic.

Activity Option 1
Share from articles, news reports or your own reading the cultural understanding of love. If possible, share a story that demonstrates agape love.

Activity Option 2
Ask the group to briefly list well-known love stories they have read or seen portrayed in the media. Discuss the difference between these love stories and the story of God's sacrificial love.

God's Truth (30–60 Minutes)
- As you work your way through the lesson, assign verses to be read aloud by volunteers. Work through the lesson question by question.
- Pinpoint some of the false concepts about love and clarify the aspects of God's love.

Concluding Activity (10 Minutes)
- Divide class members into small groups and discuss *unnamed* examples of types of people that they know that are hard to love. Please emphasize that the people mentioned must remain anonymous. For

example, rather than referring to the person by name or title (i.e., brother, mother-in-law, coworker, etc.), suggest they say something like: "There is a person with whom I must deal nearly every day who is always negative and critical of everyone else."

- Pray for God's ability and grace to help them love these difficult people.
- Ask members to find a partner to pray for them to develop a Christ-like love and to overcome the unloving behaviors they listed in question A (p. 84).
- Suggest that they continue to study God's Word with a small group or at least with another person to keep them accountable.
- Close in prayer.

SUPPLEMENTAL ACTIVITY

LOVE, THE FINAL FRONTIER
Read 1 Corinthians 13:1-13. Then have group members do the following:

- List at least three things that *do not* exemplify Christian love.
- List at least three things that *do* exemplify Christian love.
- What can you do to activate more of God's love in your life?

Read Revelation 19:6-10 aloud. The wedding feast of the Lamb is the beautiful picture the apostle John gives us of heaven, when the Bridegroom, Jesus Christ, and the Bride, the Church, are united in a glorious heavenly ceremony. Discuss the following:
1. In verses 6, 7 and 10, what activity precedes and follows the wedding supper? How does that activity relate to love?
2. How does the marriage supper of the Lamb present an appropriate image for God's love for His people and His people's love toward Him in return?

RESOURCES FOR CONTINUING THE JOURNEY

The following resources are available from Gospel Light for further study:

Sharing Jesus by Douglas Shaw

This is a reproducible resource that trains believers to effectively communicate Christ to this post-Christian culture. It contains 6 sessions that are expandable to 12 sessions that clarify the message of Jesus Christ, explain God's plan to use ordinary believers as His messengers, examine the target audience and their misconceptions about Christ and Christianity, and lay down the guidelines for personal witnessing.

What the Bible Is All About® by Henrietta Mears

This best-selling book is a one-volume commentary on the whole Bible that traces the common thread of Jesus from Genesis to Revelation. There are various other forms of this resource available: *What the Bible Is All About® King James Version*; *What the Bible Is All About® New International Version*; *What the Bible Is All About® Quick Reference*; *What the Bible Is All About® for Young Explorers* (children's edition); and *What the Bible Is All About®* video seminar.

There are also leader's group study guides that survey the Bible in one year. These are available in four reproducible volumes with 13 sessions in each volume:

> *What the Bible Is All About® 101: Old Testament,*
> *Genesis—Esther*
> *What the Bible Is All About® 102: Old Testament,*
> *Job—Malachi*
> *What the Bible Is All About® 201: New Testament,*
> *Matthew—Philippians*
> *What the Bible Is All About® 202: New Testament,*
> *Colossians—Revelation*

You can keep updated on the best resources available. Like many other Christians, believing for God's kingdom to be extended here on earth, it is the author's prayer that masses of people will find salvation through the Lord Jesus Christ and become growing Christians who have an effective witness. To acquire a copy of a current list of books, videos and other relevant materials, send a stamped self-addressed envelope to:

Douglas Shaw
P. O. Box 276384
Sacramento, CA 95827
Phone: 916-362-8401
Fax: 916-362-3625

Any other correspondence pertaining to the ministry may also be mailed to the same address.

APPENDIX A

HOW THE BIBLE IS ARRANGED

THE OLD TESTAMENT

THE FIRST AGREEMENT OR COVENANT GOD MADE WITH HIS PEOPLE, ISRAEL.

The Law: Genesis to Deuteronomy—the early history, the commandments and laws of the Jewish people

History: Joshua to Esther—Judges, prophets and kings of Israel

Poetry: Job to Song of Solomon—poetry, wise sayings and songs

Major Prophets: Isaiah to Daniel—prophecy concerning the future of Israel, the coming of the Messiah and end times

Minor Prophets: Hosea to Malachi—further prophecy concerning the future of Israel, the coming of the Messiah and end times

THE NEW TESTAMENT

THE NEW AGREEMENT OR COVENANT BETWEEN GOD AND ALL PEOPLE.

The Gospels: Matthew to John—the life, death and resurrection of Jesus Christ

History: Acts—the growth of the Early Church and the ministry of the apostles, Paul and new disciples

Letters/Epistles of Paul: Romans to 2 Timothy—instructions on the Christian life written to the Early Church

Letters/Epistles of others: Hebrews to Jude—instructions on the Christian life written to the Early Church

Prophecy: Revelation—God's plan for the end times, heaven and hell

APPENDIX B

---•---

THE PROBLEM WITH THE GODDESS

Many people have taken to addressing God in such terms as "She," "Father-Mother" or "Divine Parent." How should we talk about the parenthood of God? Is God male, female or neither male nor female?

The God of the universe, who exists beyond the limitations of human rational capacities, has chosen to reveal Himself primarily, but not exclusively, as Father and as King (see Matthew 23:37; Luke 13:34; Isaiah 49:15; Psalms 17:8; 36:7; 57:1; 61:4; 63:7; 91:4); not as Mother or Queen, or even as It. Here are some reasons why:

- On the practical level of moral formation, fatherhood is more demanding than motherhood. Fathers demand obedience, threaten punishment and establish standards. Where the role of fathers is diminished, society suffers.
- Further, a strong patriarchal deity is needed to counteract evil men and nations. Feminist "reimaginings" of God that magnify femininity undermine the idea that God will ultimately overcome evil.
- We can see, then, that God's revealing of Himself primarily in male metaphors is not an accident and is not just an arbitrary choice. Rather, God intends to teach us fundamental truths of our existence and our relationship to Him.

The Bible teaches that men *and* women are created in God's image (Genesis 1:26,27), and that fact gives women equal dignity to men. When it comes to parenthood, it is important to remember God's *whole* nature is reflected in the nurturing character of a mother and the protective character of a father.

APPENDIX C

OTHER TITLES AND NAMES FOR JESUS CHRIST

Advocate—1 John 2:1
Author and Perfector of our faith—Hebrews 12:2,3
Chief Shepherd—1 Peter 5:4
Counselor—Isaiah 9:6; 28:29
The Gate—John 10:7,9
The Good Shepherd—Psalm 23; John 10:11-15
Head of the Church—Ephesians 1:22,23; Colossians 1:17,18,24
The great I AM—Exodus 3:14; John 8:58
The King of kings and Lord of lords—Revelation 17:14
The Lamb of God—John 1:29; 1 Peter 1:18,19; Revelation 13:8
The Resurrection and the Life—John 11:25,26
The Light of the World—John 8:12
The True Vine—John 15:1-8

Action Step: Set aside a separate time to read each passage and meditate on the meaning of each of these titles or names of Jesus in your life. After reading and meditating, prayerfully ask the Lord to show you how to apply what you learn to your life.

APPENDIX D

THE PROBLEM WITH REINCARNATION

God clearly tells us to get spiritual guidance through His Word and His Holy Spirit. However, many people today are seeking spiritual guidance for their present life through understanding their past lives, having bought into a "soft" western interpretation of the eastern religious idea of reincarnation. What they do not often take into account is the "iron law of karma and reincarnation." The following story illustrates the desperate condition of those who believe in reincarnation.

The old, dying man barely noticed the jostling of the stretcher as his sons and nephews bore him over the steep steps leading down to the Ganges River. He was remembering how much sorrow he had seen in his short 53 years. He also knew in his present *karmic* state, he was so far from perfection that it would be hundreds of thousands of lives yet for him before he could come close to reaching *moksha* (the release from reincarnation and absorption into the infinite).

For the law of *karma* and reincarnation is an iron law. Whatever good you get in this life, it is because you have earned it in past lives. Whatever bad you get in this life, it is a payback for the bad you have done in past lives. You have no one else to blame—it is all your own fault. In this *mandala* of *karma* and reincarnation, there is **no** grace or help from above; there is **no** forgiveness. You, and only you, can save yourself. The only way out of the cycle is to accept your fate, bear the penalty for the "sins" of your past lives, and perform the labor over and over and over again. Only the holiest of the holiest of the holy people attain *moksha*, or salvation. Becoming your own "god" is a terrible, lengthy and lonely job.

The old man was just one of tens of thousands of Hindus every year who—racked by the hopelessness of thinking that their souls are bound into the *mandala* of births, deaths and rebirths—travel to the holy city of Varanasi in the hope against hope that if they can somehow manage to die in Varanasi, be cremated on the shore of the Ganges and have their ashes sprinkled on the waters of the Ganges, then, perhaps, if the rituals have been correctly performed and the gods are not in a bad mood that day, they can be released from the endless *mandala* and their souls will find rest.

How would the Christian message "you must be born again" be good news to a Hindu?

How does the Hindu idea of being "born again" differ from the Christian understanding of being "born again"?

How could the dynamic message of the gospel of Jesus Christ be "translated" to speak to someone who honestly acknowledges that he or she has sinned against God's holy law, yet believes in the iron law of *karma* and reincarnation?

APPENDIX E

———◆———

WORLDVIEWS AS FAITH SYSTEMS

Everybody has a worldview! A person's worldview is the way he or she understands and interacts with the world. It is a set of assumptions that is in a lot of ways very similar to religious faith. It is a "big picture," such as, *There is one God who created the heavens and the earth*, or *There is no God whatsoever, and there is no "reason" why any of us are here other than chance*.

This study has assumed throughout that there are several sometimes competing or even overlapping worldviews in our North American culture that at their core conflict with the gospel.

These worldviews may be summarized as follows:

1. There is a kind of popular American worldview that says, whatever works is "true." This worldview does not have much use for philosophy or religion, unless that philosophy or religion can improve one's happiness in this life. This worldview is in one sense very old—"Eat, drink and be merry, for tomorrow we die"—and represents our consumerist culture very well.

2. The faith of the modern naturalist or scientific worldview is that the material world is all there is. Reality and knowledge are defined by what we know from our five senses and how our five senses are enhanced through science. In this worldview, there are no Spirit or spirits that we can "know"; all claims to knowledge of Spirit or spirits are seen as subjective experiences within a person's head and not verifiable. In this worldview, science is seen as completely rational and objective.

3. The postmodern worldview takes as a given that there is no absolute truth, but many "truths"; that there is no binding morality for all time, only social conventions of

morality defined by those in power. In short, there is no absolute right and wrong; everything is relative. The postmodernist is also skeptical of the modernist's claims to be rational and objective. The postmodernist does not believe that truth contradicts nontruth, but that all truths are part of reality.

4. The New Age view combines elements of Hinduism, Buddhism and nineteenth-century occultism (spiritism, or calling on the spirits of the dead). It is polytheistic and syncretistic in the sense that it is open to and borrows from spiritual experiences from all cultures—for example, there has been a rise in paganism and nature religion among some New Agers. It is pantheistic in the sense that it usually asks people to recognize that they are God or at least part of God (connected to God) in an integral way. Reincarnation is a common belief among New Agers.

In contrast to these four worldviews, the biblical worldview teaches that there is a God in heaven who created the universe and everything in it, and is involved with His creation and cares for the earth and the people on the earth. It contends that the spirit world is just as real as the material world, if not more so. The biblical worldview insists that no one except God knows the absolute truth completely and that God communicates His truth to those He has created through nature, through history, through the Bible and preeminently through His Son.

Identify examples of each of the above worldviews from your own experience in our culture.

APPENDIX F

———— ◆ ————

HOPE FULFILLED

Old Testament Expectation	New Testament Fulfillment
Day of the Lord (judgment) Psalm 110:5	Day of Jesus Christ (Second Coming) 1 Corinthians 1:8
Day of the Lord (blessing) Isaiah 11:11	Day of Jesus Christ (First Coming) Philippians 1:6
God's Son's righteous reign Psalm 110:1	Jesus reigns at God's right hand Matthew 26:64; Acts 7:55
The Promised Land, flowing with milk and honey; Exodus 3:17	Heaven Hebrews 11:8-10
The Sabbath (the "Rest of God") Exodus 16:23	Resting from trying to earn heaven Hebrews 4:9
Jerusalem (Zion), the mount of the Lord Isaiah 10:12	The heavenly Jerusalem Hebrews 12:22
Mount Sinai; terror Exodus 19:16	Heaven; faith and peace with God Hebrews 12:18-20
The Tabernacle and the Temple Exodus 25:9—27:21; 1 Kings 5:5—6:38	The Church, temple of the Holy Spirit 1 Corinthians 3:16; 6:19
The altar 1 Chronicles 28:18	The heavenly altar Hebrews 9:1-14
Daily sacrifices for sins Numbers 29:6	One sacrifice for sins, once for all Hebrews 10:11-18
Aaronic priesthood Exodus 28—29	Jesus, the High Priest of our faith Hebrews 4:14-16
Moses as servant and friend of God Exodus 4:10; 33:11	Jesus as Son of God Hebrews 3:1-6
Old Covenant written on stone Exodus 20: 1-17; Deuteronomy 9:10	New Covenant, written with Jesus' blood on the hearts of believers Hebrews 8:10-12; 9:15
Messiah to come Isaiah 7:14; 9:6,7	Messiah came and will come again! John 1:14; 4:25,26
Escape from slavery in Egypt Exodus 1—12	Escape from the tyranny of sin and Satan 1 Corinthians 10:1-14
Messianic peace (religious) Isaiah 40:1-5	Peace with God and man (First coming) Ephesians 2:17
Messianic peace (political) Psalm 110:1	Peace to the whole earth (Second coming) 1 Corinthians 15:24-26
All nations come to Jerusalem in the Messianic age Isaiah 2:1-5	Church goes to whole world, under the power of the Holy Spirit Acts 1:8